CW00649789

History of Canada

A Captivating Guide to Canadian History

© Copyright 2021

All Rights Reserved. No part of this book may be reproduced in any form without permission in writing from the author. Reviewers may quote brief passages in reviews.

Disclaimer: No part of this publication may be reproduced or transmitted in any form or by any means, mechanical or electronic, including photocopying or recording, or by any information storage and retrieval system, or transmitted by email without permission in writing from the publisher.

While all attempts have been made to verify the information provided in this publication, neither the author nor the publisher assumes any responsibility for errors, omissions or contrary interpretations of the subject matter herein.

This book is for entertainment purposes only. The views expressed are those of the author alone, and should not be taken as expert instruction or commands. The reader is responsible for his or her own actions.

Adherence to all applicable laws and regulations, including international, federal, state and local laws governing professional licensing, business practices, advertising and all other aspects of doing business in the US, Canada, UK or any other jurisdiction is the sole responsibility of the purchaser or reader.

Neither the author nor the publisher assumes any responsibility or liability whatsoever on the behalf of the purchaser or reader of these materials. Any perceived slight of any individual or organization is purely unintentional.

Free Bonus from Captivating History
(Available for a Limited time)

Hi History Lovers!

Now you have a chance to join our exclusive history list so you can get your first history ebook for free as well as discounts and a potential to get more history books for free! Simply visit the link below to join.

Captivatinghistory.com/ebook

Also, make sure to follow us on Facebook, Twitter and Youtube by searching for Captivating History.

Contents

Introduction – Canada: A Work in Progress

"Human beings are works in progress that mistakenly think they're finished. The person you are right now is as transient, as fleeting and as temporary as all the people you've ever been. The one constant in our lives is change."

-Daniel Gilbert

The region of North America that we call "Canada" was at one time considered the New World's greatest frontier country. Yes, out of all of North America—meaning modern-day Mexico, the United States, Canada, the many Central American countries, and the various islands surrounding the continent—the Canadian frontier was the most challenging to settle. Mexico was the first of the three largest nations of North America to be colonized when Spanish conquistadors sailed from Europe to subdue the Aztecs, Maya, and Incas.

The midsection of the North American continent was then tackled by other western Europeans who slowly pushed west from the eastern seaboard. The northernmost section of North America, however—that great land of Canada—was the last to be subdued. Even today, there are sections of Canada in the far north that remain largely unexplored.

But as challenging as Canada was to settle, the attempts of doing so go back quite a ways. It has long been believed that even before those aforementioned Spanish conquistadors trailblazed through the Caribbean, Mexico, and Central America, the Scandinavian Vikings of the 11th century established a toehold on Canadian shores. The Vikings are said to have discovered the North American continent by accident, as they were lost and caught in a bad wind storm. As a result of this, a group of Viking navigators found themselves in Nova Scotia.

They did not know where they were, and they certainly did not grasp the significance of their landing. But neither did Christopher Columbus when he landed in the Caribbean. Columbus, after all, was seeking a water route to India, and he initially thought he had landed somewhere near the eastern Indian subcontinent. It's for this reason, of course, that he called the inhabitants he encountered "Indians."

Many incredible discoveries have indeed occurred as a result of mishaps and erroneous mistakes. And the discovery of the North American continent is most certainly one of them. The entrance of Europeans to the Americas would change both the Old World and the New World for good. Many staple crops and products that the rest of the world takes for granted were first discovered in the Americas.

Imagine, for example, a world without tobacco. From a man in Istanbul, Turkey, smoking a hookah to a teenager in Japan absentmindedly tossing a spent cigarette on the sidewalk, none of these things would have been possible without the discovery of the Americas and its indigenous tobacco crop. In fact, cigarette smoking is so ubiquitous and has been for centuries that it is hard for some to imagine life without it.

Yet, prior to retrieving tobacco from the Americas, such things were not known to exist in other parts of the world. And from the perspective of indigenous First Nations people roaming the lands that would one day become Canada, neither did the horse. Yes, as much as Native American warriors riding on horseback has become an ingrained image, horses themselves were not a part of their life until the Europeans reintroduced them to the continent. However, this is a debated topic amongst scholars, as some believe that the natives had access to their own horses during the wave of colonization. Most historians seem to believe that horses had gone extinct and that the European visitors suddenly flooded North America with horses, as well as guns and steel tools—all things that the indigenous residents of Canada came to desire.

As much as we might despair over the tragic outcomes that occurred as a result of contact, there were indeed benefits for both involved. And in at least the early days of Canadian settlement, trade between the original inhabitants and the newcomers was booming. In fact, the early Canadian economy was almost entirely built around the fur trade.

Local tribes knew that if they hunted animals and skinned them of their furs, they could turn around and trade them to European settlers for horses, guns, steel pots and pans, or whatever else they may have wanted. The locals had become so used to this routine that it was common for a ship just arriving on the North American shores to be greeted by excited residents raising their best furs on long wooden poles, indicating that they were ready to trade.

It was on this mutual beneficial understanding that much of early Canadian settlement would be built. As things progressed, however, it obviously did not end up going as well for the local tribes as it had in the beginning. But by then, it was too late. Their old ways of life had diminished, and they had become dependent on trade with the newcomers. They also began to be entangled in their own struggles and wars.

The French-Canadian settlers began to team up with Native American tribes in order to offset their small numbers against the more numerous British who began to encroach on Canadian territory. These happenings would eventually culminate in the French and

Indian War, which France would ultimately lose, causing almost all of their Canadian holdings to be handed over to the British.

This would be the end of French overseas power in Canada, but the French Canadians would remain. Britain now had its hands full with trying to create some semblance of unity between the two distinct communities of English-speaking Canadians and French-speaking ones.

Although this union has become much closer through the years, it is a relationship that is still evolving. This was evidenced when Quebec citizens nearly voted to leave Canada altogether in a 1995 referendum. Canada is a wonderful place with room to grow, but it is definitely still a work in progress. This is the history of how that progress has been made.

Chapter 1 – The General Geology of Canada

"I grew up on the edge of a national park in Canada—Timberwolves, creeks, snow drifts. I really did have to walk home six miles through snow, like your grandparents used to complain."

-Dan Aykroyd

The Canadian landscape is about as diverse and dynamic as it gets. Canada clocks in at over three and a half million square miles, with Russia being the only country on the planet able to boast greater terrain. Canada is so large that it has full access to both the Atlantic and the Pacific, as well as the Arctic. The northernmost reaches of Canada, however, are a virtually uninhabitable wasteland of snow and ice, whereas southern Canada features immense forests and wildlife.

Canada boasts a wide variety of trees, with spruce, pine, and, of course, maple trees immediately coming to mind. These trees are hardy specimens that can survive cold spells as well as dry periods in which precipitation might be scarce. Canada also has rich farmland but not quite as much as its southern neighbor, the United States.

Only about 5 percent of Canada is farm-worthy, whereas about 40 percent of the United States is utilized for farming. Nevertheless, Canada makes use of that 5 percent, and with its lower population of just 38 million—compared to the United States of America's 330 million—Canadians have more than enough crops to make do.

Geologically speaking, the land of Canada was highly influenced by the last Ice Age. During the last full-blown Ice Age, Canada, at different periods, was almost completely covered in ice, as glaciers advanced all the way to the midwestern regions of what's now the modern-day United States. Canada experienced several cycles in which this glacial ice covered up most of its territory before it retreated back to the Arctic.

As the ice sheets retreated, they created great gouges in the land, which today make up Canada's numerous streams, rivers, and lakebeds. The site of great glacial retraction in the center of modern-day Canada is known as the Canadian Shield. After the ice left, an immense plateau of igneous rock was exposed. Such land is not so great for farming, but it is a real boom for miners seeking out precious minerals.

And here, in this abundant stretch of rocky land, plenty of copper, silver, nickel, and even gold can be found. This resulted in famous mining towns such as Ontario's "Sudbury" popping up, and these were centered almost entirely around the excavation of the precious minerals from the Canadian Shield. This sparsely settled region is just about as fantastic and remote to Canadians as it is to anyone else. This, of course, is due to the fact that the vast majority of Canada's population live just outside of the Canadian Shield in the coastal regions and southern Canada.

Of those aforementioned coastal enclaves, one of the greatest is on the west coast of Canada, and it makes up a geologic feature called the North American Cordillera, which reaches (at least geologically speaking) from Alaska all the way to Arizona, bristling with mountains of various heights. These mountains quite literally cast a shadow and result in plenty of cloudy precipitation along Canada's western coast. The mountains also keep the milder coastal air from reaching the interior, creating a pocket of warmer climate on the west coast of Canada that cannot be found after crossing these powerful and majestic mountain ranges. Most of the Canadian Province of British Columbia, as well as a section of the Yukon, can be found along the North American Cordillera.

Another major geological feature of Canada is the Great Plains. This is a stretch of flat steppe land that stretches from the Ontario region to the Rocky Mountains. It spans some 695,000 square miles of Canada's southern interior. This stretch of Canadian soil boasts a continental climate of rather chilly winters and hot but very brief summers. The powerful Saskatchewan and Mackenzie Rivers snake through this region for several thousand miles.

This land is great for prairie dogs and grazing animals, which roam fields that stretch as far as the eye can see. For human beings, though, it is the St. Lawrence Lowlands of southeastern Canada, nestled above the Great Lakes, that provides the most comfort. This region has a good climate, arable land, and a vast supply of water. In this region, one can find the populous eastern Canadian cities of Montreal, Quebec City, and Ottawa.

Just east of the lowlands, you get into Canada's branch of the Appalachians—a mountain range that stretches from Canada's Newfoundland all the way to Georgia in the United States. The whole mountain range is full of rivers, lakes, and streams in abundance, as well as some decent farmland to boot. However, the region is most known for its wooded terrain, as well as its rich mineral deposits.

Of course, the coldest and least populated portions of Canada are the north, and they make up the taiga and arctic climates of Canada. The taiga is a very cold region of northern Canada, and it is known for its harsh winters. The taiga, nevertheless, sports the great boreal forest, which is just a part of one massive forest system of the Northern Hemisphere that rings the entire planet. The boreal forest in northern

Canada is connected to the same tree system in Russia and Scandinavia. Just imagine a ring of hardy, snow-covered coniferous trees circling some of the northernmost landmasses on the globe.

This northern region of Canada makes up a massive part of the country, but only a very small population of people can be found here. One of the main outposts in the taiga region is Yellowknife, a town that boasts a population of just under twenty thousand people.

Farther north, where the environment is even more extreme, one reaches the portion of Canada that is actually situated in the Arctic. The Arctic region doesn't have trees as the taiga does, and it sports a landscape of uninterrupted ice and snow year-round. You might find some lichens and moss clinging to arctic rocks, but this climate is far too harsh to support even the hardiest of trees.

Nevertheless, the Arctic region does have some interesting wildlife, such as the Arctic fox, the snowy owl, and, of course, the polar bear. This is the general geology of Canada in a nutshell, although there is always more to discover.

Chapter 2 – Canada before the Arrival of the Europeans

"We owe the Aboriginal peoples a debt that is four centuries old. It is their turn to become full partners in developing an even greater Canada. And the reconciliation required may be less a matter of legal texts than of attitudes of the heart."

-Romeo LeBlanc

The part of the world we call Canada has a history that long predates the arrival of the Europeans. The name Canada itself is said to have been derived from a term that the Iroquois used: *Kanata*, which roughly translates as "settlement" or "meeting place." The Iroquois, of course, were just one of several Native American civilizations that inhabited the Canadian portion of North America.

The indigenous people groups that existed prior to European discovery were many and diverse. Some of the more ancient civilizations are believed to have already come and gone prior to the days of Christopher Columbus. Although some tribal leaders may tell you that their people have been a part of Canada since the dawn of time, it is generally believed that the first of what have been termed the First Nations of North America arrived around fifteen thousand years ago.

Much of what we know of these first residents of Canada comes from archaeology and oral legends since none of the Canadian tribes (as far as we know) had established a method of writing. Most mainstream archaeologists believe that the first Native American tribes arrived in North America and ultimately what we know today as Canada around fifteen thousand to perhaps even twenty thousand years ago at the end of the last Ice Age.

It is believed that these ancient explorers may have crossed over between continents on a land bridge that connected Eurasia to Alaska. Although the vast bulk of this land bridge is now submerged under water, the remnants of this bridge today can be seen in the form of Alaska's Aleutian Islands, which are a chain of islands that stretch toward Siberia.

The theory of a mass migration over a land bridge from Siberia has been greatly bolstered through DNA research, which has found a strong link between many Native American groups and the East Asians of the Mongolia and Manchurian regions of northeast Asia. However, there are those who have asked the question—could it be that this migration happened in the reverse of what archaeologists think?

It has been suggested that perhaps ancient indigenous Americans traveled to East Asia, where they set the foundations of the Mongolians and Manchurians and not the other way around. It is an interesting thought, but there is scant evidence that this was the case. On the other hand, there is very strong evidence that the ancient tribes of the aforementioned East Asian lands traveled across a land bridge to the Americas at the tail end of the last Ice Age.

During this period, much of the world was covered in glacial ice. The fact that much of the earth's water was frozen in pack ice resulted in a lower sea level and thus more dry land. It is believed that after all of this ice melted, the land bridge connecting Alaska with Eurasia was submerged under water. Perhaps the Native American tribe that bears the strongest evidence of this connection is the Inuit. The Inuit people are a "circumpolar" tribe, and they have an unbroken chain of settlements from Siberia to the North American Arctic to Greenland.

At any rate, the North American continent for these first people groups was much different than it is today. At the end of the last Ice Age, fifteen thousand years ago, North America was full of a wide variety of animals that simply no longer exist. Giant, fur-covered elephant creatures called wooly mammoths roamed the plains. There were also fearsome big canine critters called dire wolves. Another entirely unique animal inhabitant was the ground sloth.

The Native Americans interacted with and hunted these animals. In fact, there is evidence of the ground sloth having confrontations with humans shortly after humanity's first arrival. There are fossil records featuring several human footprints and sloth footprints imprinted together in a manner that suggests a struggle between human aggressors and a sloth, which appears to have been attempting to raise itself up and defend itself.

With indications such as these in the fossil records, it has been suggested that these sloths and other Ice Age-era animals may have actually been hunted by these early human settlers all the way to extinction. Other theories suggest that maybe they died off due to natural climate change or perhaps a combination of both climate change and overhunting.

Most of the new arrivals to America at the end of the last Ice Age eventually marched south, following the Cordillera Mountain range of Canada's west coast to the more temperate regions. As the ice began to retreat farther north toward the Arctic about ten thousand years ago, these Native American tribal groups began to move steadily north and east to settle most of what we have come to call Canada. This process is believed to have been completed about seven thousand years ago when the glaciers had fully retreated and when the temperatures were roughly equivalent to what we have today.

In the Yukon, one of the oldest Native American settlements was found. In a spot called Old Crow, we find a settlement that archaeologists date back to roughly fifteen thousand years ago. This is important since this coincides with the time period that most scholars believe the nomadic tribes first made their trek from Eurasia to North America.

These early settlers braved the elements and hunted large game such as deer, elk, and even the huge wooly mammoth. Such powerful beasts provided both warm fur coats and a large portion of meat, which enabled these early Americans to survive the harsh winters of the Canadian frontier. And there is archaeological evidence that tribal settlers were developing more complex communities and, along with hunting and gathering, began to regularly conduct fishing operations on the western coast by 8000 BCE. Then, as now, Canada's western shores have plenty of salmon for any would-be fishermen.

As tribal groups migrated east, there is evidence of the gradual advancement of tools. The earliest settlers used chipped stone tools. But soon there were tribes with better polished stone tools and weapons. Then, by 3000 BCE, there is evidence of tribes using copper as the main resource for crafting their various utensils.

Coinciding with these developments was the widespread use of canoes, which, in turn, led to the frequent trade of goods between various tribes. The use of pottery was also widespread by 1000 BCE, especially near the Great Lakes. Around Canada's portion of the Great Lakes, tribal groups began to transition away from a hunting culture to an agrarian one, causing widespread farming to become more prevalent.

It was here that signature crops such as maize were developed and widely distributed among local tribal groups. Maize, of course, is an important agricultural fixture, and it was first developed much farther south by the advanced indigenous civilizations of Mexico. The crop eventually spread from Mexico to the northernmost section of the

North American continent (i.e., Canada). And yes, by 1000 BCE, maize was indeed a common enough crop, even in Ontario.

Complex religious beliefs also began to flourish during this period, as is evidenced by the vast burial mound complexes that began to dot the landscape. Archaeology can only tell us so much about why the locals buried their people in these mounds. But by the great lengths that they went to create and preserve them—well enough, in fact, that we can still see them to this very day—it is quite clear that these mounds were very important to their society. The most extensive of these mounts is the Manitou Mounds, which can be found in Ontario.

Many of these complex societies remained intact for thousands of years—some all the way until post-Columbian contact. It was around this time that the Iroquois tribe came to prominence around the Great Lakes region. The Iroquois, sometimes classified as a tribal confederacy, were a large group of indigenous tribes who all spoke the same Iroquois language and who had banded together to control a large swathe of the northeast. Their lands ranged from modern-day Virginia, Pennsylvania, and New York in the south to Ontario in the north. The political system of the Iroquois Confederacy was complex, consisting of local councils headed by village chiefs. They were independent states in themselves yet all bound together for mutual defense. This confederacy of the Iroquois is considered one of the most elaborate indigenous social structures present in North America.

Interestingly enough, it has even been recognized that the original Articles of Confederation, which banded the Thirteen Colonies together in their opposition to Great Britain, actually drew some inspiration from the Iroquois system. The tribes of the Iroquois brought together several tribal units into one common front, and they were united for defense and the general welfare of all members. The Thirteen Colonies initially united as a confederacy for much the same reason.

The most visible feature of Iroquois society was, no doubt, their famed longhouses. These long wooden structures, which were typically twenty feet in width and as much as two hundred feet in length, could be found all over the Great Lakes region. The longhouses were used for communal dwellings as well as a place for the local leaders to discuss the most pertinent political matters of the day.

Just imagine several local representatives of various tribes of the confederacy meeting in a longhouse to debate pressing matters affecting the tribal groups as a whole. Once the Europeans arrived on the scene, much of these debates would be in regards as to how the confederacy should handle these strange newcomers.

The Iroquois lived on both their crops and wild game, and these two labors were typically divided between males and females, with the men primarily being the hunters and the women primarily tending to the crops. The three main crops grown by the Iroquois are sometimes referred to as the "Three Sisters." These Three Sisters were the Iroquois staple crops of beans, squash, and maize. Supplementing the Iroquois diet was a steady number of fish, which were most abundant in the springtime.

Of course, the Iroquois were just one of many indigenous people groups in Canada, but their importance cannot be understated since they would eventually become the most important power players when the post-Columbian Europeans eventually made their way to Canada.

Chapter 3 – The Viking Attempt to Settle Canada

"Canada has always been there to help people who need it."

-Justin Trudeau

Brash explorers from the reaches of Scandinavia (northern Europe) known as the Vikings were making major inroads by the 9th century. Although they are perhaps better known for their bloodthirsty raids launched against Britain and continental Europe, the Vikings—despite their bloodlust—were also incredible sailors and navigators.

The Vikings are, indeed, an often-misunderstood group. For centuries, they have been stereotyped as belligerent pagan holdouts who suddenly swarmed down from their northern outposts on an unsuspecting Europe. They were described as bloodthirsty barbarians who ruthlessly raided villages and churches in places like Britain and France, thus leaving us today with one-dimensional characters at best.

But while it is true that the Vikings were capable of incredible violence, one of the main catalysts of this violence often goes unmentioned. The Vikings, you see, actually believed that they were at war with Christianity. And furthermore, they didn't feel that they were the ones who started the conflict. That credit went to Holy Roman Emperor Charlemagne (r. 800–814 CE), who began to forcibly convert the pagans of Denmark. This was conversion by the sword, plain and simple, and it sparked an armed conflict.

During the course of the conflict, Charlemagne's men actually set fire to a sacred tree of the Norse called the Irminsul, which was an earthly representation of Yggdrasil or the "tree of life" of Norse mythology. According to Norse prophecy, once Yggdrasil fell, Armageddon (or as the Norse called it "Ragnarök") would begin. Thus, the Vikings literally believed that Charlemagne had triggered Armageddon by cutting down their sacred tree, and it is really not much of a coincidence that they began descending upon Europe shortly thereafter.

The Vikings basically thought, "Well, if you burn my sacred tree, then I will burn your sacred church!" And that is what they did. It should be noted, however, that there are some scholars who contend the Vikings attacked places that seemed vulnerable, such as monasteries, as they would provide easy loot for little work.

The Vikings themselves, of course, would eventually find a peaceful means to convert to Christianity, with most of them becoming Christians by the 12th century. But in the meantime, there was a lot of fighting, as well as exploring, that the Vikings would take part in.

In around 825 CE, the Vikings left Norway to establish a settlement in the Faroe Islands, which lay in the waters north of Scotland and west of Norway. From this launching pad, the Vikings were then able to discover another sizeable island about four hundred miles west of the Faroe Islands. Settled by the Vikings in 860 CE, this new island was named "Iceland." It was a little over one hundred years later, around 980 CE, that the Vikings leapfrogged from Iceland and went even farther west, bumping into an even larger landmass—a place they called "Greenland."

According to the Norse sagas, Viking explorer Erik the Red was the champion of this cause. It has been said that he left Iceland and landed on the southwestern coast of Greenland. It was also Erik the Red who supposedly gave Greenland its name. He called it thus, thinking that such an appellation would serve as a great marketing tool for settlement since green pastures sound attractive. However, Greenland is not all that green; in fact, it is even more ice-covered than Iceland!

As an interesting aside, it was around the time that Greenland was founded that the Scandinavian equivalent of parliament—the Althing—was having vigorous debates about whether or not to leave the ancestral faith of the Norse religion for Christianity. With that in mind, it could be that some diehard Norse believers were seeking new lands such as Greenland and then maybe even North America for similar reasons that Protestant Christians would later come to the Americas—for religious freedom.

Even more fascinating to ponder as a possible motivating factor is the Norse legend of Valhalla. Many have the misconception that Valhalla was simply Viking heaven, a non-physical dimension that the souls of the slain Vikings passed on to. But this is not the case. The Vikings believed that Valhalla existed as a tangible piece of land far across the mysterious waters west of the traditional Norse lands of Scandinavia.

Taking that into consideration, one can better grasp what might have inspired some of these Vikings to make all of these dangerous westward journeys across uncharted waters. Some may have actually believed they were searching for Valhalla itself.

At any rate, once Greenland was tamed by the Vikings, they used it as a staging area to head even farther afield. According to Norse lore, a Viking merchant by the name of Bjarni Herjólfsson sailed into a bad storm on his way from Iceland to Greenland. He was knocked so far west that he ended up on the shores of a completely unknown landmass.

Bjarni had no idea where he was, but he quickly corrected his route to get to Greenland as planned. When a Norseman by the name of Leif Erikson heard of this account, he was intrigued enough to look into the matter himself. Leif Erikson was actually the son of the famed Erik the Red. It is for this reason, of course, that his name was Erikson, or Erik's son.

Leif Erickson and his fellow Viking mariners would use the clues given by Bjarni, and they would find their way to a place they called Vinland. Most scholars today believe that Vinland was actually the northeasternmost coast of North America. They also landed on a rocky island they called Helluland, which seems to correspond with present-day Baffin Island. Leif's group is said to have spent the winter of 1001 in what today is known as Newfoundland.

It has been said that Leif spent the rest of the year at this outpost without much incident before heading back to Greenland. After Leif's return to Greenland, his brother Thorvald is said to have made his own trip to the newly discovered territory of Vinland in 1004. It is thought that Thorvald Erikson departed from Greenland with a group of some thirty men. This group landed in roughly the same location where Leif Erikson's encampment had been.

According to the Viking sagas, Thorvald was apparently a rather violent and aggressive fellow. They say that after stumbling upon a group of indigenous people resting under "three skin covered canoes," he launched an unprovoked attack against them. It remains unclear why he would do such a thing. Perhaps he considered it a preemptive strike, cutting down potential nearby aggressors before they could strike out against him and his followers.

If so, it was most certainly a cold-blooded calculation on his part, as he cared very little for the lives he took. But even if this was his aim, his efforts were a miserable failure. Thorvald and his men did indeed kill eight of the nine men they encountered, but one lone survivor managed to escape. And this was all it took to bring the wrath of a whole tribe down upon these Viking interlopers.

The Vikings hid behind some hastily constructed barricades put up around their settlement, and they managed to hold their assailants at bay, but Thorvald himself was killed in the process, making him the first European to die in the Americas. An arrow sailed through the fortifications and struck him down right where he stood. Nevertheless, the rest of the crew managed to survive the winter before heading back to Greenland in the spring.

The Norse sagas then speak of yet another ill-fated expedition in which a man by the name of Thorfinn (yes, quite a few Vikings had "Thor" in their name), along with his spouse Gudrid and several others, landed in North America. It was shortly after their arrival that Gudrid gave birth to a child named Snorri. If Norse legend is to be believed, this could be the first European baby born in the Americas.

Initially, the expedition went quite well for the group. And unlike their predecessors, these Vikings managed to set up some rather peaceful relations with the local tribes. Instead of fighting with the local inhabitants, these enterprising Norse began to trade with them. Trading food and furs were fine, but once the local tribes began to ask for steel weapons such as broadswords and heavy battleaxes, Thorfinn ordered his followers to deny them these trade goods.

His reasoning was understandable enough. Thorfinn feared that if he handed over their best weapons to the locals, the Vikings would lose any military advantage they might have had. It would be like the United States handing over its best stealth aircraft and nuclear submarines to China for the sake of "friendship." Most pragmatic military leaders would not do such a thing, and Thorfinn, no matter how friendly the locals were, was not about to do that either.

According to the sagas, the local tribes took offense to this, and they began to conspire against the Vikings. A group of them then apparently tried to steal from the Vikings what they would not trade, sparking an altercation that left one of the local tribesmen dead. In a virtual repeat of what had happened to Thorvald several years prior, this triggered a tribal avalanche of aggression, as a huge number of the natives descended upon the small Viking camp to avenge their fallen comrade.

Despite being outnumbered, the Vikings were able to hold off their attackers due to solid fortifications and—thanks to Thorfinn—their superior arms. Even so, they knew it was only a matter of time before they would be driven into the sea, so taking a hint, the Viking survivors loaded up their ships and headed off to Greenland once again.

The Viking experiment in North America didn't last very long. It is said to have taken place for just a few years—perhaps as brief as being from the year 1001 to the year 1007. The most concrete evidence of Viking habitation comes to us from Newfoundland, for it was in Newfoundland's L'Anse aux Meadows that intact Norse housing was uncovered, along with several other souvenirs of Viking settlement.

There was even evidence of iron smelting. Iron is not believed to have been known to the indigenous groups, but it is rather indicative of Norse settlement, as they had a penchant for fashioning mighty steel blades for their broadswords. This archaeological evidence seems to correspond to the Norse sagas that tell the tale of settlement in what is now Canada.

Chapter 4 – Early English and French Colonies

"If the national mental illness of the United States is megalomania, that of Canada is paranoid schizophrenia."

-Margaret Atwood

The story of how Christopher Columbus sailed to the New World of the Americas, reaching the Caribbean in 1492, is fairly well known. The much lesser-known expedition of John Cabot (the Italianized version of his name is actually Giovanni Caboto) on behalf of Britain took place in 1497. This Italian sailor was quite skilled, and the English monarch—King Henry VII—apparently had full confidence in him.

Good old King Henry had famously advised Cabot to "seek out, discover, and find, whatsoever isles and provinces" and claim them for England. Cabot sailed out of the British port of Bristol that year and ended up landing on the old stomping ground of the Vikings' Newfoundland. Cabot was authorized to claim any "newly" discovered land for England, and that is what he did, officially declaring Newfoundland to be the property of the British crown.

This, of course, was done no matter what any of the local tribes might have thought about the matter. The area was sparsely populated, and if any of the locals happened to catch a glimpse of the strange newcomers planting the British flag, they probably wouldn't have thought too much of the act itself besides being amazed by the alien nature of the visitors. For them, the lands of Newfoundland didn't have a single owner but were the ancestral homeland for all of the local tribes.

In truth, the British claim was largely a means of fending off other Europeans from attempting inroads in the region. The action was meant to notify their European peers that this little chunk of Canada was now in British hands. And even though Britain would not be able to develop any permanent settlements there for several years, just the notion that Britain had staked out a claim was considered to be of great national importance for the country.

Early on, one of the most bountiful resources to be discovered in Newfoundland was a rich supply of fish. The fish were so plentiful that mariners came back with tales of ships getting stuck in enormous swarms of them. At one point, Cabot is said to have had baskets dropped down under the waters only to have them pulled up absolutely loaded with these aquatic animals.

This part of the ocean was so full of fish that fishing wasn't even a challenge. The spot where Cabot's ship encountered this huge abundance of marine life was near the continental shelf in a particularly shallow section, which just so happened to be a breeding ground of cod. The fishing trade off the shores of Newfoundland would indeed become quite lucrative.

Besides finding new land for England, the English, like many Europeans, were still eager to find a westerly route to India. Even though both Columbus and Cabot had proven that there was a landmass between East Asia and western Europe, no one had yet figured out just how large this landmass was. At this point, it was anyone's guess, and it was commonly believed that the new land being discovered was much smaller than it turned out to be.

As such, explorers like Cabot figured that a quick expedition to the other side of this newfound land (well, it was called Newfoundland for a reason) would lead them right to East Asia. The land that lay between Europe and Asia was viewed as nothing more than a mere speedbump. Of course, we know that getting from the Atlantic coast of Canada to the Pacific coast is not a quick trip by any means.

Cabot, however, persisted in this pursuit. He led his expedition down into the Gulf of St. Lawrence, and he followed the waterway, hoping to find a direct passage to India or even China. Needless to say, he did not find what he was looking for. Cabot's explorations came to an end in 1498 when four out of five ships on his latest expedition were lost. One managed to limp back to Ireland, but nothing was ever heard of John Cabot again; to this day, it is not known what happened to the Italian explorer. King Henry VII himself perished shortly thereafter.

France, in the meantime, made its first forays into exploring North America in the year 1524. Like so many others, France was also interested in finding a quicker, westerly route to India. The French, just like the British—and consequently the Spanish via Christopher Columbus—utilized a skilled Italian navigator, a man known as Giovanni da Verrazzano.

By this time, Spain had leapfrogged from its discoveries in the Caribbean to settlements in Florida. John Cabot, in the meantime, had marked the outline of Newfoundland for the British. Interestingly enough, it was Giovanni Verrazzano who was convinced that there must be a water route between these two far-flung points. Giovanni obviously had no idea that both Newfoundland and Florida were part of the same continent.

Nevertheless, Giovanni persisted. He actually made his way to the spot where modern-day North Carolina is. There, his eyes played some tricks on him, convincing him that he saw a large "ocean-like body of water" just above where North Carolina would be. This was just a trick of the lighting, however, and just like Cabot, Giovanni would return to France with no new route to India.

Nevertheless, this trip added greatly to the knowledge of the correct contours (at least after Giovanni realized his mistake) of North America. French exploration would be put on hold shortly after this expedition, as wars erupted with the Hapsburg dynasty in continental Europe. France would not get back into the game until about a decade later, in 1534, when explorer Jacques Cartier sailed out of the port of Saint-Malo in the northwestern French region of Brittany.

His expedition consisted of sixty-one men, and they spread across two different ships. It took them a little over a month to reach Newfoundland. Jacques was not too thrilled with the ice and snow of the region, and he remarked that perhaps it was "the land God gave to Cain." He dubbed it thus in reference to the biblical narrative of Cain being exiled to the "Land of Nod." Just like John Cabot before him, Jacques sailed into the Gulf of St. Lawrence and then preceded to make his way to Prince Edward Island.

From here, he headed on up to Chaleur Bay, the body of water that separates the lands of Quebec from that of New Brunswick. While passing through this body of water, the expedition encountered some locals from the Mi'kmaq tribe, who were apparently waiting for them on the shore. It has been said that the locals became quite excited upon seeing them, and they held up furs on wooden poles, indicating that they would like to trade them for other goods.

This was a clear indication that these people had traded with visitors before and knew the routine. After this encounter, Cartier's expedition made its way to Gaspe, where they found more native inhabitants—this time members of the powerful Iroquois. It is said that the French readily handed out glass beads, knives, combs, and other trinkets to the Iroquois tribesmen. This was ostensibly done to win their friendship, which would then allow the explorers to use the locals to show them around.

But what happened next does not seem all that friendly. It has been said that the crew of Cartier's ship deliberately sought out and abducted a couple of the local chief's sons. These two Iroquois princes were then forcibly impressed into service for France and worked as regular scouts during subsequent missions. As brutal as this practice was, this was actually a recurring pattern with these voyages.

As well as forcing locals to serve as guides, the indigenous people were often brought back to the expedition's point of origin simply as living proof that the crew had traveled where they said they did. Yes, there was no denying that Jacques Cartier had landed in a strange new land when he had an Iroquois prince standing at his side upon returning to France. Cartier made his return trip to North America in 1535, landing off the shores of modern-day Quebec.

In fact, shortly after this landing, Canada got its name. At this time, one of Cartier's Iroquois guides made reference to the land as being *Kanata*, the Iroquois word for "meeting place" or "settlement." Cartier began using the word for the entirety of the land itself, and it stuck. From that point forward, the northernmost chunk of North America in its entirety would become known as "Canada." This expedition also named a cove St. Lawrence, and eventually, the aforementioned Gulf of St. Lawrence had acquired the very same name.

Despite the previous forceful taking of captives, the French actually maintained pretty good relations with the local Iroquois of Quebec. The Iroquois valued the French for the steel utensils that they were able to trade their furs for.

It was initially a fairly beneficial arrangement for both. The French were able to profit off of the fine furs, selling them back in Europe for great profit, and the Iroquois were able to get steel goods such as steel pots for cooking and steel knives for hunting and warfare—objects that they otherwise would not have had. Due to their solid relations with the Iroquois, the French were able to travel through their lands virtually unimpeded, and by that October, they had made their way farther north to the much larger Iroquois settlement of Hochelaga.

At the settlement, it is said that over one thousand locals greeted the explorers. It is quite obvious that word had already gotten around about their presence. You might think that these Frenchmen, who were greatly outnumbered and knee-deep in a foreign land, might have had some misgivings. But due to the friendly relations developed through trading, coupled with the far superior French arms—hardly any of the locals had guns at this point—the French were fairly assured they could handle almost anything.

The situation was obviously much different than what the Vikings supposedly encountered several centuries prior, as their one bad encounter was enough to drive them back to Greenland. Unlike the Norse, the French were quite confident in their efforts. Supposedly as Cartier confidently climbed up to the top of a huge hill, he named the spot Mount Royal. This is ultimately where the name of Quebec's future settlement of Montreal came from.

Interestingly enough, Cartier still had not given up on the old idea that a quick trip across this new frontier could possibly lead one to the shores of East Asia. He gazed toward the rapids of the St. Lawrence River, which was west of the settlement. Perhaps he thought that it just might somehow lead him to China. Whatever the case may be, he referred to them as the Lachine Rapids, or, in other words, the "China" rapids.

Cartier and his crew ended up spending the winter in Quebec. During this extended stay, the French apparently managed to overstay their welcome as far as the Iroquois were concerned. Growing suspicious of some of these expeditions upriver, the Laurentian branch of the Iroquois had become frustrated with the French. But a much greater threat than any local hostility for these French explorers was the elements. It was a brutally cold winter that year in Quebec, and by January, the French were dealing with ships nearly becoming encased in ice. And on the ground, their encampments were often covered in several feet of snow.

As they shivered in the cold, sickness broke out, especially bad cases of scurvy from a pronounced lack of vitamin C. It was only after learning to use a Native American cure of boiling bark and leaves of the white cedar tree and drinking the concoction that the crew's illness was alleviated. Upon recovering, the French expressed an interest in heading west to visit the land of the Saguenay tribes.

The Frenchmen had heard rumors that the Saguenay had copper deposits, and they wished to learn more. However, they ran out of time, and by the spring of 1536, they had to head back to France. Domestic turmoil and then a war with Spain ended up putting further expeditions on the backburner, and France would not return to the New World until 1541. On this return trip, Cartier would lead an expedition west of Quebec to check out that fabled land of the Saguenay, as well as take another stab at gaining access to the Northwest Passage (a sea route that connected the Atlantic and Pacific).

Upon their return to Canada, this French group of explorers split into two teams. Cartier led one team of explorers himself, and they headed upriver to the region of Cap-Rouge. They disembarked here, and some 150 crew members set up camp. They brought cattle, began an agriculture project, and constructed dwellings. They endured a rough winter, and they were occasionally attacked by local tribes. Some thirty-five of their number are said to have died. The results of this experiment were so dreadful that Cartier was ready to head back come springtime.

With a boat loaded up on quartz and pyrite (fake gold), Cartier returned to France. He was apparently under the false impression that he had diamonds and real gold in his possession. It has been said that he was so thoroughly ridiculed for his ignorance that the phrase "Faux comme un diamant du Canada," or, as it is in English, "fake as a Canadian diamond" became a widespread phrase in France.

After Cartier's return trip, the other half of the expedition arrived at the settlement of Cap-Rouge. This group consisted of two hundred colonists led by explorer Jean-François de La Rocque de Roberval. They tried their best to literally weather the storms of the Canadian winter, but fifty of them would die before it was through. Roberval would then return to France later that summer. Due to a lack of results and further turmoil on France's political front in Europe, further exploration was sidelined for the next few decades.

In the early 1600s, however, a new French explorer—Samuel de Champlain—began to pick up where all the others had left off. He took part in the Grave expedition, arriving at the St. Lawrence Valley in late 1603. They were accompanied by Pierre Dugua de Mons, a man who was leading the fur trade. This cast of characters sought to create a foothold in Canada's interior. Pierre eventually led his crew to what we now call Nova Scotia, which is just south of Newfoundland, setting up shop in the region in 1604. This led to the establishment of Port Royal and the beginnings of a long-term French-Canadian colony called Acadia.

It was a rough first winter, and it has been said that seventy-nine of these early French colonists perished prior to the first thaw. However, the French stayed, and by 1606, their condition had stabilized. Nevertheless, shortly thereafter, Pierre made the decision to move on due to what he viewed as a lack of profitable enterprise. During the French stay at Port Royal, much effort had been made to extract precious minerals, yet not much was gained. The ever-present side mission of finding the Northwest Passage had also failed to render any results. The port even seemed lacking as a trading post to trade furs since just about any European competitor could sail right through and take business from the French without ever having to put down any roots in the region at all. It was for all of these reasons that the expenditure of sustaining this outpost began to seem too costly to maintain.

Port Royal would ultimately be revied by Jean de Biencourt de Poutrincourt et de Saint-Just (yes, he had quite a long name) several years later as a self-sufficient farming community. And soon thereafter, the Jesuits would establish a Catholic base for French missionaries. Port Royal would ultimately be destroyed by the British in 1613 after a deadly skirmish erupted.

In the meantime, Champlain and company made their way back to the St. Lawrence Valley in 1608. Their goal was to create a solid foothold in the interior of Canada and to keep other European competitors out. Champlain oversaw the construction of a new settlement, which was situated around several fortified wooden structures. The fortifications were then further fortified by walling it off within a wooden stockade.

These colonists were far from home and could be waylaid by an outside force at any time without any additional recourse or aid to assist them. As such, they had to make sure that their settlement was as impregnable as possible. The narrow strait that surrounded the settlement was only crossable by a lowered bridge. It was this feature that inspired the French to name the settlement "Quebec," a French variation of the word *Quebec*, which was used by the local Algonquian tribe, which roughly translated meant "narrow passage."

But although the French were fairly safe in their fortress in the middle of the Canadian wilderness, they weren't immune to succumbing to sickness and the elements. And that winter would be another rough one, with some twenty-eight French colonists perishing.

The French managed to establish friendly relations with the local Montagnais tribe. The Montagnais were themselves looking for an ally since they were in a bitter war with the Iroquois. The Iroquois possessed the military advantage and were wreaking havoc on the Montagnais. The Montagnais wanted to use the French to regain the upper hand, which they hoped to do so through trade. They sought steel tools as well as French muskets, which they could use against their adversaries. Pleased with the French trade, the Montagnais then went a step further and actually requested the French to actively join them in their fight against the Iroquois.

Eager to keep up the partnership, the French ultimately decided to take the Montagnais up on their proposal. Thus, in 1609, Champlain led a joint Montagnais/French force against the Iroquois. They ended up taking on a band of some two hundred Iroquois, and although the French and Montagnais were outnumbered, the French muskets proved decisive in cutting through the enemy positions and causing the Iroquois to retreat.

By aiding their tribal allies, the French were, in turn, aided by being given important information about the interior of the land, as well as unique tools and strategies to survive the elements. For example, the locals introduced the French to snowshoes and toboggans, which helped them get around even in the midst of bad winter storms. But perhaps most importantly, their resourceful tribal allies began to regularly supply the French with plenty of hunted game, which was more than enough to sustain them during long winter stretches.

The natives also taught the French colonists the fine art of making maple sugar, which would become a staple of the settlers' diet. Champlain soon sought to expand his alliances further by making contact with another powerful tribe. In 1610, he sent out feelers to the mighty Hurons. After contact was made, the French actually established a hostage exchange with the Hurons.

The practice sounds dreadful, but it was quite common in the ancient world, and it was a known practice among North American tribes. It involved one party sending one of their own in exchange for a member of the other party. So, in this case, the French sent one of their own young men, a man named Étienne Brûlé, to live with the Huron while the French took into their midst a young Huron called Savignon. It was through their special guest and further subsequent relations that the French settlers came to know the Huron people fairly well.

They discovered that this tribal group boasted quite a healthy population—it is said to have been thirty thousand strong—which was stationed around one of the Great Lakes, the one we now call Lake Huron. The French also discovered that the Huron tribe was indeed powerful enough to take on the mighty Iroquois. The Huron had a mastery over trade in the Great Lakes region of Canada, dominating the trade from Lake Huron to Lake Superior and all the way up to James Bay. In fact, the Huron presence was so important that their native tongue had become the main lingua franca of the region simply as a means for the other tribes to conduct trade.

It was for all of these reasons and more that the French decided to establish formal relations with the Huron so that they could use them as a valuable cog in their own international wheel of trade networks. And by the 1620s, the Hurons supplied the French with the vast majority of the furs they received. Working as a local intermediary, the Huron gathered up as many as fifteen thousand fur pelts from surrounding tribes each year to trade to the French.

The fact that the Hurons became the primary intermediary in this trade network put them in a powerful position over their indigenous peers, as it meant that the other tribes were forced to trade their furs to the Hurons in exchange for valuable French goods, which the Hurons themselves had received from the French in the process of conducting trade. Once this "middleman" relationship was established, if the locals wanted French steel, they had to go to the Hurons to get it. And if the French wanted furs, they, too, also had to go to the Hurons.

Yet this strong alliance between the French and the Hurons had its downside since it meant that the French were obligated to engage in military operations against the Hurons' greatest threat—the Iroquois. This would set the stage for future confrontations with not just the Iroquois Confederacy but also with the British, for it was the British who would ultimately align with the Iroquois against their rivals—*the French.*

Chapter 5 – The Rise of New France

"Canada has a passive-aggressive culture, with a lot of sarcasm and righteousness. That went with my weird messianic complex. The ego is a fascinating monster. I was taught from a young age that I had to serve, so that turned into me thinking I had to save the planet."

-Alanis Morrissette

Although the British touched down in Canada as early as 1497 through the efforts of John Cabot, their real success story occurred in 1607 with the founding of Jamestown in what is modern-day Virginia. This colony had its ups and downs, but it gradually became strong. By the 1620s, it boasted a large population, and the people excelled in agriculture, making it highly attractive for more future colonists to settle there.

It was the success of Jamestown that made the French government realize that something was lacking with its own colonization project in the Canadian territory. It was decided that the French colony was far too dependent on the fur trade and that it needed to diversify its investments. With this in mind, King Louis XIII of France had his top court official—Cardinal Richelieu—send out the word that the

Canadian colony of New France needed to wean itself off of its addiction to the fur trade.

It was made known that in order for the colony to stop being so dependent and become more competitive with the other European powers, it needed to develop its own strong farming and industrial base in Canada. It was through Cardinal Richelieu that a new colonial expedition was organized through the so-called "Company of One Hundred Associates."

This company was made up of one hundred investors who pooled their finances together behind efforts to maximize the profits of New France, as well as to spread religious missions. The Company of One Hundred Associates pledged to send around four thousand settlers to New France, as well as to promote missionary activity, over the course of a fifteen-year period. But it was right as this revamped colonial effort was gaining traction that war erupted between England and France.

Thus, in the backdrop of these colonization efforts, British pirates raided French settlements. In 1627, the British even managed to seize French vessels, which carried some four hundred would-be French colonists, interrupting their attempt to settle Canadian territory before they even managed to land. Under immense pressure, Champlain himself was defeated by the British in July of 1629 and forced out of Quebec.

It appeared that French Quebec was all but lost, but due to political intrigues between the British heads of state, an agreement was eventually hammered out to return the territory to France. As it so happens, the English king, Charles I, had actually wed French King Louis XIII's sister, and he used the capture of French territory as a bargaining chip to force the French king to pay for his sister's dowry. The French king did so in 1632, and that was enough for the British to relinquish the seized territory back to France.

Champlain returned to Quebec in 1634, where he returned to what he knew best—the fur trade. He established a new trading post for furs in the region of "Trois-Rivières in the year 1634. Samuel de Champlain passed away the following year, and with his passing, the stewardship of this outpost was handed over to the French Catholic missions, with the Jesuits taking a leading role.

The Jesuits, of course, had a primary mission of converting the native inhabitants to Christianity. This they did with varying degrees of success. The locals had a hard time understanding Christian concepts, and it could be furthermore argued that perhaps the Jesuits did not present the tenants of their faith in the most understandable of fashions. Without wading too deeply into the metaphysical realms of faith, the basic concept of Christianity is that humanity had fallen astray on a spiritual level, prompting God to manifest himself in a physical form through the person of Jesus Christ.

Yet if the Jesuits, like many preachers even today, just went around repeating key catchphrases without explanation, it might have been hard for the locals to follow. Without the proper metaphysical backing, they probably became confused with what the French preachers were talking about. And what might have otherwise been a powerful spiritual narrative about a creator God who loved his creation so much that he would take on a human form to rescue them had devolved into incomprehensible talk of blood and crucifixion.

To their credit, the Jesuits did eventually attempt to relate to their Huron audience on a more personal level and discovered similarities in their beliefs that could be used for some common ground. Both the Hurons and the Christians, for example, believed in the supernatural and its influence on everyday life. The Jesuits were able to use this natural inclination toward the supernatural that the Hurons already had and redirect it toward Christianity.

The Jesuits respected the Huron rituals of fasting and vision quests, recognizing it as being similar to Catholic fasting and communion. Also of importance was the fact that the Huron firmly believed in an afterlife, which gave the Jesuits familiar territory to develop upon by preaching on the Christian belief in heaven.

However, as the Jesuits were about to gain trust and make inroads, they managed to unwittingly shoot themselves in the foot. They unknowingly carried on their shoulders strains of viral infections from Europe to which they themselves were largely immune, yet the indigenous people had no immunity for. During the course of their missions, the Jesuits unknowingly spread smallpox to the local population. The disease absolutely devastated the Huron communities. Interestingly enough, the Huron were soon making the distinct connection between the visiting Jesuits and the arrival of the disease.

Always seeing things through a supernatural lens, the Hurons became convinced that the Jesuits were somehow using evil magic against them. They believed that the fact these priests were not getting sick while their presence seemed to sicken so many others was an indication that they had some kind of malignant, supernatural power. This led to the Hurons going from mostly confused and indifferent to the Jesuits preaching to becoming altogether intolerant.

Even so, the Hurons knew they could not expel the priests outright, as they would risk losing trade with the French, upon whom so much of their survival now depended. It was only when the Iroquois began to dip into the trade market as well, doing business with both English and Dutch traders, that the Huron situation seemed just about impossible. The Iroquois now had better and more plentiful guns than the Huron, giving the Huron leadership some serious doubts as to just how beneficial their relationship with the French remained.

In consideration of the aggressive conversion being forced upon them by the French Jesuits and their weakening position against their traditional rivals (the Iroquois), some Huron leaders were greatly concerned. One of them even went as far as to remark, "You tell us that God is full of goodness, and then, when we give ourselves up to him he massacres us. The Iroquois, our mortal enemies, do not believe in God, they do not love the prayers, they are more wicked than the Demons—and yet they prosper; and since we have forsaken the usages of our ancestors, they kill us, they massacre us, they burn us—they exterminate us, root and branch. What profit can there come to us from lending ear to the Gospel, since death and the faith nearly always march in company?"

Considering all of the misfortune that had befallen them, the Hurons were understandably enough at their wits' end with the tenuous position in which they had found themselves. In the end, however, they opted to continue to throw in their lot with the French, feeling that switching sides at this point would only bring more destruction to their community. This decision to stick with the French set the stage for a confrontation between the Hurons and the Iroquois in the spring of 1649.

For it was around this time that a huge Iroquois army attacked a major Huron settlement, killing or taking prisoner nearly four hundred Hurons. Those who were not killed were compelled to join the Iroquois as adopted members, and through them, further raids were led. Interestingly enough, these Huron turned Iroquois warriors carried an especial hatred for the Jesuit priests, and upon attacking French settlements, they captured many Jesuits and systematically tortured them in what was, in their eyes, revenge for all of the trouble they believed these priests had wrought upon their people.

The ultimate defeat of the Hurons led to a power vacuum in the region, which the Iroquois promptly sought to fill themselves. But the Iroquois did not set themselves up to become an ally of the French; instead, they began waging war against them. The French were now without their main native ally, so they were left to themselves to take on this resurgent threat. In the early 1650s, several skirmishes between French settlers and Iroquois ensued. The only good thing for New France during this period was that the actual French population had finally become substantial, reaching over three thousand by 1662.

In 1663, King Louis XIV of France decided to aid the stature of this growing colony. He declared the settlement to be an official royal province of France. This status enabled the colony to take on a much greater prerogative. Since it was now a province, New France would have its own governor, meaning a direct channel to the king of France. But most importantly, this distinction meant that more military troops could be deployed. And in 1665, one thousand troops were sent to the province of New France.

The province was also supplied with horses. This was a momentous occasion, for the colonists' native allies had never seen these animals before. Yes, as much as Native Americans came to be associated with horses in later years, the horse was not known to them at this time (although it is believed their ancestors once rode them). Horses were brought to various parts of North and South America by Europeans, and they rapidly multiplied from there.

The indigenous allies of the French were said to have greatly admired these majestic animals and referred to them as the "French moose" since North America's homegrown moose was the closest thing that these indigenous tribesmen could associate with the horses being imported to their lands. The following year, the French took their growing army to take on an Iroquois Confederacy member, a tribe called the Mohawks.

The Mohawks were unable to handle this large force, and they ended up surrendering to the French in 1667. The Seneca, another tribe of the Iroquois Confederacy, bargained for peace just a few years later. These developments proved that the colony of New France could stand on its own. And by 1671, the French had taken control of the entire Great Lakes region. Their new native allies, the Algonquians, then moved down to take over the former territory of the Hurons.

The Iroquois, for a change, knew that they were beaten, and after the British entered into a peace treaty with the French in 1697, the Iroquois followed suit by forging a peace treaty in 1701. It has been said that the establishment of this treaty with New France's old foe was quite an affair, one that lasted for several days. During the signing itself, over a thousand representativeness from the Iroquois, who stood in for some forty different nations, had made their way to Montreal.

Rather than simply signing a piece of paper, these members of the Iroquois Confederacy made sure to give their own lengthy regards and words of wisdom. After these moments of reflection were through, several gifts, as well as former prisoners of war, were exchanged. It was only after all of this great festivity had run its course that the treaty was actually signed on August 4th, 1701.

However, the general peace and tranquility of New France would be shattered ten years later when the British decided to launch a major naval attack on France's holdings in Canada. First, an attack was launched against Acadia in 1710, which was followed up by an attack the following year on Quebec. This latest war with the British would last for a couple more years before the two parties signed the Peace of Utrecht in 1713.

This treaty allowed France to keep most of its territory, but the French had to agree to give the region of Acadia to the English. It was a tough price to pay, but this treaty would give France some thirty years of peace before the next round of fighting would begin.

Chapter 6 – The Next Round: France and England Compete for Dominance

"Canada has two emblems—the beaver and the maple."

-John W. Dawson

After the signing of the Peace of Utrecht in 1713, Canada was fairly evenly divided between the French and the British. The British were given the territories of Nova Scotia, Newfoundland, and sections of Rupert's Land in addition to what they already had. The British colonies now stretched all along the eastern seaboard of North America, from Newfoundland to the Florida border, with Florida still being controlled by Spain.

France, in the meantime, may have lost some territories, but the colonies it maintained began to prosper like never before. With less worry of fighting and dying in endless wars, the colonies' population exploded, and by the 1750s, New France boasted around fifty thousand settlers. This was a great improvement from the previous century, which saw numbers barely over one thousand.

These settlers were also much better provided for, as each man had his own piece of property complete with pigs, chickens, cows, and even some horses. The French Canadians became quite proficient at growing crops, such as wheat, for food, and they chopped firewood for warmth. There was also abundant wildlife to hunt, and fishing always produced stellar results.

Despite the cold winters, New France had become a land of plenty. As the settlers learned to better adapt, even the cold was not much of a hardship. They had learned how to build houses that were good at keeping in heat, as they were designed with a fireplace right in the center of the dwelling. The colonists also began making clothes that maximized heat retention, which eased their burden of having to move about on cold days. They even learned to pick up some fun pastimes in spite of the weather, such as ice skating and riding on sleds.

But not all was well for all of the French Canadians. For those who remained in lands that the British had seized, such as Nova Scotia, life was not always so easy. The English were naturally suspicious of their new French-Canadian subjects, and multiple times, they tried to get the French Canadians to sign an oath of loyalty.

Things came to a head in 1755 when it was demanded that they sign a pledge agreeing that they would take up arms and fight for Britain if war should ever break out. The French Canadians did not want to battle their own friends and relatives in nearby French-controlled territory should the two nations come to blows, and they flatly refused to sign.

The British authorities were not pleased, and they decided to evict the French outright. That August, it was announced to the French under British jurisdiction who refused to sign the oath that "Your lands and tenements, cattle of all kinds and livestock of all sorts are forfeited to the Crown with all other your effects, saving your money and household goods, and you yourselves to be removed from this province."

After being given this ultimatum, it is said that over the course of the next few years, some ten thousand French Canadians were kicked out of British-controlled territory. Of these, a sizeable chunk headed all the way down to the French-controlled Louisiana territory. The rest were pushed far and wide, with some settling in other British-controlled colonies, some in other French-controlled regions, and still others heading back to France itself.

War would once again erupt between Britain and France in 1756, as the Seven Years' War had begun to be waged on the European continent. By this point, the French and British colonies had already been fighting amongst themselves in what is known as the French and Indian War. Nevertheless, this war is often seen as one of the theaters of the Seven Years' War. This meant that the French stronghold of Quebec would become the main base for a buildup of troops, as well as additional French expatriates. The director of this military buildup was the governor of New France—the Marquis de Vaudreuil. The captain of the ground forces was a man named Louis-Joseph, also known as the Marquis de Montcalm.

Despite his name, the Marquis de Montcalm was not very calm. In fact, he was known for being agitated and short-tempered. And it was not long before he and the governor were butting heads. Most troubling for the French war effort was that these two men greatly disagreed on strategy. Montcalm wanted to use standard European battle tactics of simply marching an army in formation straight for the enemy. Vaudreuil, a man who was born and raised in North America, wanted to utilize the same kind of hit-and-run attacks that were so successful for the Native American tribes. Instead of charging headlong at the enemy, Vaudreuil wanted to use more cunning tactics to catch their British opponents off-guard. Nevertheless, despite the arguments over tactics, the war proceeded.

Initially, the French and their Native American allies did fairly well at repulsing the British from the interior of Canada. France was also beating the British on land in Europe. It was at this point that the

British decided to pull out their trump card—the Royal Navy. Britain had the best navy at the time, and the British decided that if they couldn't best the French on land, they would do it by sea. They sent a powerful fleet to one of France's best Canadian ports—Louisbourg—and began to bombard it mercilessly in 1758.

Even so, the port held out for a couple of months, and despite the wreck and ruin all around them, the only thing that finally defeated the French defenders was their own hunger. When the besieged settlement's food began to run out, they realized that they had no choice but to surrender. It was not long after this victory that the British set their sights on their next main target in North America—Quebec.

The British invasion of Quebec began in early 1759 when some twenty-nine warships bristling with artillery, along with fifteen thousand troops aboard various other attack craft, sailed up the St. Lawrence River and came face to face with the mighty fortifications of Quebec. Montcalm was in charge of Quebec's defense, and he tried a variety of tactics to fend off the intruders.

First, he sent a small group of fire ships toward the approaching British fleet. These were wooden craft purposefully set ablaze with the intention of sending them flying into an opponent's craft so that they might catch fire. However, the ships missed their mark, and to the delight of the British, they merely burned up some distance away. Montcalm desperately tried to get the French king to send reinforcements in the meantime, but France was too busy dealing with the war in Europe proper. He was only able to send a few hundred auxiliaries at most to bolster the defense of New France.

It is worth mentioning that such slights were not new for the French colonies, and many of the French subjects were already growing weary of their French overlords' seeming disregard for them. Considering the trajectory of this sentiment, one could only speculate that had the British not seized the French colonies in North America for themselves, the French colonists just might have staged a revolution of their own against mainland France.

At any rate, faced with an outright enemy invasion in 1759, such things were the least of these colonists' concerns. The British began to bombard Quebec on the night of July 12th. In the United States, the bombardment of the American Revolution is commemorated on the 4th of July with fireworks because, after enduring the worst that the British could dish out, with their "bombs bursting in air," the American revolutionaries' "flag was still there." However, for the French Canadians in Quebec, they were not as lucky, and this British bombardment on July 12th really took its toll. The British launched firebombs that tore through homes, churches, businesses, and military barracks alike, burning them to the ground in fiery explosions. They also launched repeated mortars and cannonballs that pounded Quebec's fortifications.

Although rubble and ruin lay all around them, the French held on for a few more months. But when their food supply began to run low, they seemed to be in for a repeat of the last defeat at the hands of the British. The British then dealt the final blow on September 12th when a British force of around three hundred men made landfall at L'Anse-au-Foulon. They found a wilderness path that allowed them to sneak around the coastal fortifications. After walking some 150 feet up to the clifftops, they were able to easily overpower the French defenders, who were unprepared for an all-out assault.

At the time of this breach, the main bulk of the French-Canadian forces were about an hour away. As soon as they received word of what was happening, they immediately rushed over as fast as they could. The armies met shortly thereafter, and a climactic land battle ensued. Just as the British and French were fighting to the death on the European continent, they were now fighting to the death in North America.

The battle didn't go well for the French. Montcalm himself died in the melee, and the French forces were forced to retreat into the cover of the wilderness. Rather than the French flag surviving this onslaught, on September 18th, the British flag was seen flying high in Quebec. The British were now in control of Quebec, and their most immediate problem was now what they were going to do with it.

After all, they were now the stewards of a wrecked and ruined city, which contained a frightened populace of foreign civilians. There was also the threat of disease, with outbreaks among these huddled masses not at all uncommon. The British also had to contend with French fighters from Montreal. This fortified city had not yet fallen, and a French force was being sent to try to retake the ground that had been lost to the British. This French contingent collided with the British out on the open plains in April of 1760.

The British had trouble with their artillery since it sank in the springtime mud, becoming relatively useless. The battle was pitched, but there was no clear winner. The French and British were both in need of reinforcements, so when a ship was seen arriving by way of the St. Lawrence River, both hoped that more of their countrymen had arrived. It was only when the craft unfurled a British flag that the French knew that all hope was lost. The French troops were now outnumbered, so they retreated back to Montreal. The British pursued them, and Montreal surrendered shortly thereafter.

In the aftermath of their defeat, the French were primarily concerned with the religion of the French citizens who would remain under British occupation. It was for this reason that the so-called "Articles of Capitulation" were to have a religious clause. The clause declared, "The free exercise of the Catholic, Apostolic and Roman Religion, shall subsist entire, in such manner that all the states and the people of the towns and countries, places and distant posts, shall continue to assemble in the churches, and to frequent the sacraments as heretofore, without being molested in any manner, directly or indirectly."

And with that, Canada was in the hands of the British, and this situation was made official by the Treaty of Paris in 1763, which also ended the Seven Years' War. But although the French had been defeated, there was still the matter of what to do with their Native American allies. Several local tribes had alliances with the French Canadians, and the British had to contend with those First Nations peoples who remained. Not all of them were friendly to these European newcomers.

This was evidenced by the words of an Ojibwe chief, who remarked, "Englishmen, although you have conquered the French, you have not conquered us!" And as it pertained to Pontiac—the famed chief of the Ottawa—as far as he was concerned, the war was still indeed on.

The Ottawa dreaded the arrival of the British because they tended to settle more densely than their French allies had, and they also cleared and used up more land. In addition, the Ottawa had no trade relations with the newcomers, so it makes sense that they might pine for their close relationship with their old French partners. Pontiac was not willing to negotiate with the British, and he took the fight directly to them.

He ended up launching several assaults, one of the most devastating being the one he launched against Fort Detroit, which had only recently been taken over by the British. Here, countless British troops and civilians alike met a grisly end. Pontiac's initial onslaught was quite terrifying, but he was unable to keep up the enthusiasm among his troops. Due to a variety of factors, including the outbreak of smallpox, as well as fighters losing interest and dropping out of the fight to get back to their old stomping grounds, the offensive began to stall.

Pontiac realized that he could not sustain a large enough army to drive the British out, so he finally agreed to enter into a peace treaty with them in 1766. This was the end of the fighting, and it would soon be the end of Pontiac, as one of his own disillusioned people killed him in a fit of rage over what was perceived as their defeat.

However, the British did develop an understanding with the remaining indigenous people. This understanding led the British government to forbid their subjects from establishing any unauthorized settlements in the interior (west of the Appalachian Mountains), which was traditionally considered Native American territory. With this line drawn in the sand, British Canada could have peace—at least for the moment—with its newfound neighbors.

In French Canada, in the meantime, decisions were made to ease the French Canadians' load. In stark contrast to what had happened to previous French settlers who found themselves under the dominion of the British, it was decided to give these French Canadians significant leeway. It was determined that they could keep not only their religion but also their own French civil law and even a form of governance, as they could have their own elected officials. Although they would speak French and have their own religion and customs, these citizens would be granted the same rights as all other Canadians under British rule.

These measures were finalized in 1774 in what would become known as the Quebec Act. Little did the British know that these newfound freedoms for the French Canadians would provoke unsuspected yearnings from thirteen of their American colonies just a little farther to the south.

Chapter 7 – An American Revolution and the War of 1812

"But what do we mean by the American Revolution? Do we mean the American war? The Revolution was effected before the war commenced. The Revolution was in the minds and hearts of the people; a change in their religious sentiments, of their duties and obligations. This radical change in the principles, opinions, sentiments, and affections of the people was the real American Revolution."

-John Adams

In 1775, although Britain had made peace with both France and its own French subjects, the descendants of British colonists in the Thirteen Colonies that would one day become the United States of America were seething with discontent. The Quebec Act of the previous year was seen as an insult to them since they believed it gave a small population in Quebec special treatment over the much larger population of the American (as in the original Thirteen Colonies) settlers in the Northeast. They also resented the fact that their own heavy tax burden had helped to pave the way for England's victory against France, yet they didn't feel that they received many benefits in return.

The Canadian neighbors in Boston, Massachusetts, were particularly incensed, and they staged the Boston Tea Party to show their displeasure in 1773. They dressed up as Iroquois, stormed a ship, and dumped tea into the waters in order to protest excessive taxation without proper representation.

These tensions ultimately led to the Thirteen Colonies making the fateful decision to break with Britain, and the colonists launched the American Revolution in 1775. After the war was launched, it was suddenly a "you're with us or against us" kind of moment, and many of those who wished to remain loyal to the British fled north to Canada.

The French Canadians, in the meantime, wished to stay neutral. They had only just recently patched things up with the British, and they did not have much sympathy for the rebellious Americans to their south—certainly not enough to join them in a war against what was then arguably the greatest military power on the planet. However, the general of the revolutionary forces, George Washington, could not stomach this neutrality, sensing the French posed a potentially grave threat to the revolution should the British coerce them into marching south to the Thirteen Colonies.

It was with all of this in mind that Washington rolled the dice and decided to send American forces up to Quebec to see if Canada could be taken by force. In the fall of 1775, Washington led troops over Lake Champlain and across Maine. The Americans were initially quite successful, and by the end of the year, Montreal was in their hands. The defenders, however, were able to rally, and the American siege of nearby Quebec City was not quite as successful.

One of the men leading the charge against Quebec City was perhaps the most infamous American of all time—Benedict Arnold. This man's very name would become synonymous with the word "traitor." But even though Benedict Arnold would famously turn traitor and flip to the British side, at the outset of the war, he was a formidable figure for the revolutionary cause.

Along with Arnold, another general leading the siege was General Richard Montgomery, who had arrived just in time from Montreal to add some seven hundred additional troops to the group that Arnold was leading. After the victory over Montreal, Montgomery was feeling bold. In fact, he was bold enough to declare that he would "eat Christmas dinner in Quebec City or in hell." Well, if he somehow managed to eat Christmas dinner that year, it certainly was not in Quebec City. Montgomery and his troops were still outside the walls of the city after Christmas had come and gone.

On December 30th, braving white-out conditions, Montgomery and his men managed to storm into the city, but it did not go well at all. General Montgomery passed right by a gunner's nest, and his head was blown apart as powerful muskets opened upon him. He most likely died from the terrible head wound he suffered, but even so, the shots kept coming, literally riddling the American general with bullets as his body crumpled in a bloody heap on the snow. The sight of their commander brutally dispatched like this sent a shockwave of fear through General Richard's now leaderless troops, and they immediately fled out of the city.

Benedict Arnold was now left to try and salvage the disaster. His army, like General Montgomery's, managed to enter the city, but they did not get very far after that. Arnold would get hit by gunfire, with a bullet blasting through his leg, pulverizing flesh and bone. Unable to walk, Benedict Arnold had to be taken off the field. The revolutionaries would struggle on without him, but due to a lack of supplies, the outbreak of disease, and mounting casualties, they became bogged down in street fighting.

Matters would get even worse when on May 6th, 1776, British reinforcements arrived on the scene. Unable to deal with thousands of fresh British troops, the revolutionaries were forced to retreat. In the end, Benedict Arnold, who was replaced in April of 1776, had nothing to show for his troubles but a bad leg injury and perhaps a growing disillusion with the capabilities of his fellow revolutionaries against the British.

With Quebec firmly under their control, the British would use it as a future staging ground for attacking the rebellious American colonies. France, in the meantime, officially declared itself to be allied with the Thirteen Colonies of America. The French king wished to take full advantage of the situation in a wide variety of ways. First and foremost, the French wanted to strike at their old foe by supporting the Americans. France wished to weaken and humiliate the British by aiding the Thirteen Colonies in breaking away, but it did not want to push out the British completely. It served French interests to leave Britain in control of Canada in order to be a buffer to the upstart Thirteen Colonies should they outgrow their usefulness to France.

At any rate, the Americans ultimately bested the British, and another Treaty of Paris was created in 1783, ending the war and recognizing the independence of the newly formed United States of America. As for the British holdings in Canadian North America? They would indeed remain in British hands.

Interestingly enough, after the war was over, a call went out from the British asking anyone wishing to remain loyal to the crown to come to Canada. Several did so, seeking a better life and a little plot of their own to settle in underpopulated Canada. This group of post-revolutionary immigrants is sometimes referred to as "Late Loyalists" since they only professed loyalty to Britain after the war was already over.

Many of these later arrivals ended up in a section of what was then Nova Scotia, located above the Bay of Fundy. In 1784, this settlement was turned into its own colony called New Brunswick. Just north of Maine, the boundary of this new colonial province was the St. Croix River. Since it was so close to the former Thirteen Colonies, many feared an invasion from the Americans. As such, British garrisons at New Brunswick's capital of Fredericton were always at the ready.

More big changes were on the way in 1791 when Britain divided Quebec into what it termed Upper Canada and Lower Canada. Known as the Canada Act, this act of the British Parliament divided Quebec by way of the Ottawa River, with Upper Canada being the portion upriver and Lower Canada being the piece that was downriver.

By the early 1800s, the situation had mostly stabilized, and the younger generations of Canadians and Americans had, for the most part, come to accept the status quo and were more likely to trade goods with each other and conduct commerce than to fight. In the meantime, Britain had problems of its own after the French Revolution of 1789 and the Napoleonic Wars that followed.

Britain was at war with France off and on from 1803 to 1815. In the midst of this struggle, the actions of the British began to rub the Americans the wrong way. The British supposedly sought naval deserters, and they developed a habit of randomly stopping and searching American craft just in case British deserters were on board. This "stop and frisk" of the high seas was very insulting to the Americans who had to go through it.

The so-called "*Chesapeake-Leopard* affair" demonstrated just how volatile and potentially explosive this situation had become. In 1807, an American freighter called the *Chesapeake* got the bad end of the stick from the British. The British naval craft, the *Leopard*, came across the American sailors near the shores of Virginia and demanded that they be allowed to board and conduct a search on their craft.

These sailors were perhaps a bit bolder than most. Despite the fact that they were staring down the barrels of British guns, they denied the British access to their craft. This prompted the indignant British military men to take over the ship by force. Without any apparent regard to the damage they might do, the British opened fire on the civilians, killing three in the process. Several more were wounded.

Even worse, after searching the craft, the British grabbed four men on board in order to force them into impressment. For those unfamiliar with the term, impressment was when a civilian was forced against their will to serve someone else's cause. Things did not end well for at least one of these impressed American civilians, as the British eventually had him killed.

The United States was understandably outraged by all of this, yet at the same time, American leaders were not confident that they would be able to win another war with the British. As such, the sitting president, Thomas Jefferson, tried his hand at diplomacy in order to avert a cataclysmic confrontation with Great Britain. Even so, Jefferson understood the anger of the American public. In the midst of this ordeal, he is said to have remarked, "Never since the Battle of Lexington have I seen the country in such a state of exasperation."

Americans today would no doubt be just as frustrated if they were put under similar circumstances. Just imagine a foreign power seizing an American craft in American waters and then killing and injuring several and taking hostages. It would not be viewed upon favorably, that's for sure! Yet, since this took place just a few decades after the American Revolution, no one was quite ready to pull the trigger as it pertained to British aggression. Perhaps the British had already called this bluff.

However, once James Madison became president, he decided that enough was finally enough. He spoke of the tough position he was in, of how he essentially had to choose "between war and degradation." Rather than have America be bullied and pushed around any further, he chose war. This led to a formal proclamation of war against the British Empire (Canada included) on June 18th, 1812. The War of 1812 had begun.

At the very outset, striking at Canada was seen at striking at the British. Since Canada was not as heavily populated as the United States, it was also considered an easy target. Even the previously hesitant former President Thomas Jefferson believed this to be the case. On the eve of war, he had remarked, "The acquisition of Canada this year, as far as the neighborhood of Quebec, will be a mere matter of marching, and will give us the experience for the attack on Halifax, the next and final expulsion of England from the American continent."

But neither the Canadians nor the British would be that easy to overcome. As evidenced by Jefferson's words, many at this time believed that it was in America's interest to push the British right off of the American continent. The former Thirteen Colonies were indeed destined to push out farther west, but as the young nation of the United States of America would soon learn, pushing north into Canada was not going to be a walk in the park.

The greatest advantage that the Americans had was the fact that Britain was quite distracted with its war against Napoleonic France. French dictator Napoleon Bonaparte had proved to be a thorn in Britain's side. Bonaparte had seized much of the European continent, and Britain was doing all it could to contain the threat of Napoleonic France. With Britain's hands tied in Europe, it was indeed a nuisance for the British then to have to double back to the Americas in order to prevent the United States from taking over Canada.

But the British Empire was massive in those days, and it would soon find enough reserve troops to take the war to the Americans all the same. Just like the United States was later able to fight both the Japanese in the Pacific and the Germans in Europe during World War Two, the mighty British Empire of 1812 was able to simultaneously fight a war on several fronts as well.

Britain mustered up some six thousand troops for the defense of Canada. The Americans pulled together about twelve thousand total troops from their various militias, but getting them all in an organized fighting condition was difficult. Many states that bordered Canada on the East Coast, for example, were against sending their militias to fight. They wished to remain neutral, thereby limiting the total number of troops that could be cobbled together.

Today, the United States has a federally operated standing military; back then, however, the US Army was a patchwork of state-based militias. And if certain states refused to cooperate, there was not enough centralized control back then to do too much about it.

As it pertains to Canada, the man in charge of Canadian defense was Major General Isaac Brock. Due to limited manpower and resources, Brock was ordered by his British taskmasters to maintain a defensive posture. However, Brock had other plans; he felt that rather than wait for the fight to come to him, he would take the fight to the Americans. He marched south to Fort Detroit. Fort Detroit had a few thousand troops and should have been able to fend off the smaller Canadian force fielded by Brock, which was just over one thousand in number.

Brock's group, in fact, was said to have consisted of three hundred British soldiers and four hundred Canadian troops, along with six hundred Native American fighters who were allied with the British. But what this Canadian attack force lacked in numbers, they made up for in sheer cunning.

The Native American division of the forces was led by a daring Shawnee commander by the name of Tecumseh. Tecumseh was famed for his fighting prowess and superb use of military tactics. As soon as Tecumseh and his men arrived at the gates of Fort Detroit, he decided to employ some psychological warfare. With all of his men emblazoned with terrifying war paint, he had them march right outside the fort's walls in full view of the defenders. He then had them double back a couple more times, creating the illusion that the group was much larger than it actually was. In the meantime, General Brock used some subterfuge of his own by making sure to dress his motley Canadian militia in British uniforms, making it seem that there was a large force of elite British soldiers backing up this fearsome assembly of indigenous warriors.

After this frightening display was made to the defenders of Fort Detroit, Brock sent a message to the American commander, requesting for him to surrender. Brock laid it on thick in this missive, being sure to mention that if they came to blows, he would be unable to hold his ferocious Native American allies back. Or, as Brock actually stated, "It is far from my inclination to join in a war of extermination, but you must be aware that the numerous body of Indians who have attached themselves to my troops will be beyond my control the moment the contest commences."

Brock's scheme worked. Fort Detroit was not only the home of American men at arms but also women and children. And fearing for their safety, the commander of the fort—General William Hull—caved into doubt and fear. The very next day, he ordered the fort to surrender. Without having to fire a shot, Fort Detroit was in Canadian hands.

One has to wonder if the defenders of Fort Detroit regretted their decision after realizing just how small of a group they had surrendered to. The defenders were almost twice in number as the attackers, yet they handed the keys over to these enterprising Canadians in short order.

Along with the two thousand American prisoners of war now under their charge, Brock's Canadian contingent also acquired a huge stockpile of guns and artillery. But perhaps most important for Brock was the stash of cold hard cash he acquired, as he could use it to pay his restless band of soldiers.

The United States was understandably alarmed at these happenings. Seeking to immediately recoup from the loss, they sent a regiment up to Queenston Heights and began to open fire with long-range cannons from the other side of the Niagara River. Even though it was a tough crossing, the US troops crossed the choppy Niagara and laid siege to Queenston Heights. The Canadians put up a brave fight, and Brock himself died during the exchange. The defenders were temporarily overrun, but the rest of the Canadian army rallied and were able to drive the Americans out, retaking Queenston Heights once again as their own.

After this exchange, 250 Americans were killed, and 925 were made prisoners of war in Canada. In all, the first phase of the war had gone in favor of the British and their Canadian allies. But by 1813, however, the situation had begun to change. American forces were able to occupy York (modern-day Toronto), and they caused British troops to retreat from the Niagara Peninsula, with the Brits running all the way to Burlington Heights.

It was only after the British launched a sudden assault on American positions at nearby Stoney Creek that they were able to boot the American forces out. This was followed by a skirmish at Beaver Dams near Montreal, in which members of the Iroquois Confederacy participated in a surprise attack on American positions. The Americans were soundly defeated and forced to flee from the Niagara Peninsula altogether.

The major blow to the British, however, would occur not on land but at sea when Admiral Oliver Perry was able to successfully orchestrate victory over the British during the onslaught of Put-in-Bay over the waters of Lake Erie. This was a devastating blow for the British because they were using the lake to ferry supplies.

But perhaps a worse defeat occurred when the leader of Britain's Native American allies—Tecumseh—was killed and his warriors defeated at the Battle of Moraviantown (also known as the Battle of the Thames) on October 5th, 1813. With Tecumseh's death, Britain's Native American allies were essentially knocked out of the war since no other indigenous leader rose up to lead them.

British fortunes improved in 1814 with the defeat of Napoleon (his first defeat prior to his ultimate end at Waterloo). With France subdued, Britain was able to redirect its forces to the war in America. Things then came to a head on July 25th, 1814, when British forces once again collided with the US Army on the Niagara Peninsula in a region called Lundy's Lane.

Now known as the Battle of Lundy's Lane, this fight took place with the Niagara Falls as a backdrop. Since the fighting was often hand to hand, to say that they "duked it out" is actually fairly close to what happened. In these close-quarter conditions, one of the greatest threats they faced was getting on the receiving end of friendly fire.

At any rate, the Americans got the worst end of this brutal contest and were forced to flee, leaving almost two hundred dead soldiers behind as they ran. This was a terrible defeat, and the worst was yet to come. In August of 1814, the British marched on Washington, DC, and set the capital ablaze. Both the White House and the Library of Congress were burned to the ground. The president was fortunately evacuated to Virginia, but the psychological blow was immense.

In September, the British also seized part of the eastern portion of Maine, where they created their own base of operations right on American soil. Nevertheless, the Americans were able to make a comeback, delivering a decisive defeat to the British on Lake Champlain in the Battle of Plattsburgh.

The British, at this point, were quite frankly tired of fighting. They had just finished a terrible war with France, and it was determined that fighting the Americans further was just not worth the effort. As such, overtures for peace were made, and on December 24th, the two parties entered into the Treaty of Ghent, officially ending the war. It should be noted that neither side won the war, although if a "loser" had to be named, it would have to be the indigenous people, as they lost their land and the trade they had established with the British.

Interestingly enough, even though the War of 1812 was over, General (and future president) Andrew Jackson apparently did not get the message since he would famously fight the British to a standstill in New Orleans in January of 1815. Nevertheless, the Treaty of Ghent was a milestone in North American history. The British, for the first time, recognized the USA, and they finally gave up the idea of seizing territory in Canada.

Chapter 8 – From the 19th to the Early 20th Century

"Canada was built around a very simple premise. A promise that you can work hard and succeed and build a future for yourselves and your kids, and that future for your kids would be better than the one you had."

-Justin Trudeau

Immediately after the War of 1812, Canada experienced major growth in population as well as an increase in prosperity. Some subsequent historians would attribute this phenomenon as a "postwar boon," but more recent scholars have called the notion that the war had anything to do with these developments into doubt. Besides the war, the biggest development in Canada in the first half of the 19th century was the end of the fur trade.

Since its inception, the fur trade had played a major part in the establishment of Canada and its growth. The fur trade was such a big industry that its end would have been equivalent to the end of the oil industry today. Just to give you an idea of how important the fur trade really was for Canada's economy—it is said that in the 1770s, the fur trade made up over 75 percent of Canada's export products. Yet, by 1810, that number had dropped dramatically to just 10 percent.

Needless to say, that was quite a big drop. At this point, many fur traders had no choice but to put their eggs into more than one basket. Some got into the timber business, some in railroad development, and others became shipbuilders. The timber industry proved to be the driving force that would lead Canada away from its dependence on a fur-trade-based economy.

Canada has always had plentiful lumber due to its vast forests. This dates all the way back to the Vikings, in fact. The Vikings may have very well left treeless Greenland in order to bring back timber from Canada. Having said that, timber was still a readily available resource in the 19th century, and it was ready to take the place of the fur trade. And by that same year of 1810, it was actually the lumber industry—not fur—that made up 75 percent of all of Canada's exports.

The St. Lawrence River was also bustling with shipbuilding activity, with Great Britain being the biggest client when it came to Canadian ships. Further industrialization in Canada led to a boom in textile industries, sawmills, flour mills, and a wide variety of other industrial-based manufactured goods. Much of this production, however, took place in the English-speaking settlements, leaving French Canadians out of the loop.

This naturally led to some resentment and sparked renewed interest in their independence. The Lower Canada region of French Canadians had asked for several reforms in the spring of 1837, but they were denied. This led to widespread discontent, and public protests began to mount. By summer, these protests began to turn violent, and the destruction of both public and private property took place.

As tensions mounted, the French Canadians began to form their own militia groups as they prepared for the inevitable backlash from the British and their loyalist colonial collaborators. An all-out confrontation between the two erupted on November 23rd, 1837, in what became known as the Battle of Saint-Denis.

On the British colonial side, a certain Lieutenant-Colonel, Charles Stephen Gore, led a group of men to root out the insurrection and arrest the rebel leaders in the Richelieu River valley region of Lower Canada. The rebels were found holed up in a stone house that had a good view of the open street right in front of it. This enabled the group to easily take potshots at the authorities as they approached.

In the meantime, Gore and company tried to blow the house apart with a cannon but proved unable to do so. The house stood, and their antagonists continued to fire upon them. At this point, Gore's ill-equipped bunch actually ran out of bullets and were forced to flee. This meant that the Battle of Saint-Denis was a technical victory for the rebels. However, their winning streak would be a short one since just a couple of days later, on November 25th, 1837, the colonial authorities struck back with a vengeance.

The next encounter between the two sides of this conflict occurred near Saint-Charles. This time, more British military might was added to the picture, and a contingent led by Lieutenant-Colonel George Wetherall was able to make short work of the rebels positioned around Saint-Charles. Wetherall unleashed an infantry of over four hundred troops, with an auxiliary militia cavalry said to number around twenty, along with two powerful cannon pieces.

This well-armed group faced off against approximately 250 rebels. This group was soundly defeated, with fifty-six being killed during the conflict and several more being taken as prisoners of war. This rebel defeat was followed by an even more decisive one when the British tore through rebel positions at Saint-Eustache a short time later, effectively ending the rebellion of Lower Canada in December of 1837.

The rebels' will to fight had been broken, and those who did not surrender fled as refugees to the United States. This was not quite the end of the story, however, since these rebel refugees managed to regroup and make a comeback approximately a year later. In

November 1838, they crossed back into Canada and were able to stir up yet another revolt.

However, this one was quashed even quicker than the last one. After the revolt was put down, the British authorities did not dispense punishments with any sense of mercy or leniency—they had twenty-five of the rebels summarily executed and another fifty-eight exiled to British Australia. Canada's British taskmasters were obviously not taking any chances, and they sought to yank the sentiment of rebellion out by its roots so that it would not be able to grow and fester once again.

But a more permanent political solution was needed, and so, it was decided to bring Lower and Upper Canada together with the Act of Union, which was enacted in 1840. By creating a United Province of Canada, it was hoped that the loyal English majority, which resided primarily in Lower Canada, would be able to prevent further outbreaks of rebellion. By uniting the English dominant Lower Canada to Upper Canada, it was also hoped that the English ways and sentiment would rub off on the French Canadians. The British generally believed that it was the isolation of the French Canadians that allowed thoughts of rebellion to foment.

Further adjustments occurred a few years later for Canada as a whole when the Oregon boundary dispute erupted in 1846. The British and the Americans were arguing over a region of territory that would ultimately become the Northwest of the United States. Some in the US claimed a much larger portion should be annexed to American territory at the fifty-fourth parallel, which would bring American land in the Northwest all the way up to Alaska (a region still administered by Russia at the time).

However, the British were not going to go for this, and US President James K. Polk did not wish to provoke the British at a time when tensions with Mexico over the recent acquisition of Texas were already bad enough. Polk, therefore, sought a compromise and scrapped the idea of staking a claim as far north as the fifty-fourth parallel. Instead, he sought to negotiate with the British for a claim at the forty-ninth parallel. In the end, the British decided that a war over this small portion of land would not be worth their while, and they agreed on the American compromise of establishing Canada's westernmost border at the forty-ninth parallel.

The recently United Province of Canada, in the meantime, began to strengthen its trade ties with the United States. And by the time the American Civil War erupted in the US in 1861, Canada was in a good position to benefit from it. The US federal government was suddenly looking to Canada to supply much-needed goods during the course of the conflict.

Before the Civil War broke out, Canada had experienced a push to its western frontiers. This had been the case ever since the gold rush of 1848, with settlers slowly inhabiting lands that had previously remained wild and largely deserted. Just as Canadians were expanding to the farthest reaches of western Canada, Britain sought to create a firmer, federalized union of the Canadian territory. These efforts would forge the Dominion of Canada. This was established with the Constitution Act of 1867 (also known as the British North America Act). Within this act of British Parliament, we find the statement that Canada is to be "one Dominion," which will have "a constitution similar in principle to that of the United Kingdom."

This act, although not severing direct ties to Great Britain, sought to create one united Canadian body and to give the citizens of Canada roughly the same rights as British citizens. This act linked all Canadian lands into one dominion, and it saw the largely unsettled Northwest Territories and Rupert's Land get merged with the already established provinces. Britain would have the final say over things such as foreign policy, but Canadians would control their own destiny on the local level.

This, of course, also meant that Canada would get its own prime minister. Canada's first prime minister was a man whose name comes down to us as Sir John Alexander Macdonald. Macdonald was a conservative, and he ran against a liberal adversary, whose name was George Brown.

After Canada reached its dominion status, one of the greatest efforts of localized government was to improve Canada's infrastructure. A major part of this entailed the creation of railways that stretched across Canada from east to west. Canada received another boon when Prince Edward Island joined the dominion in 1873.

The biggest problem that the Canadian government of Prime Minister Macdonald faced was the Red River Rebellion. The tumult was in regard to a large settlement of Métis, a distinct people group that had developed from a long history of intermarriage between Europeans and local tribes. The Métis had their own large piece of territory carved out in Rupert's Land, situated around the Red River Valley and in the vicinity of the Hudson's Bay Company outpost of Fort Garry. When settlers from the eastern Canadian provinces began to settle in this region, trouble began to emerge. Not wishing to be swallowed up in the Canadian dominion, a local Métis leader, Louis Riel, rose to prominence and created what was termed a provisional government of their own.

Prime Minister Macdonald was surprised by these developments, but he took a highly pragmatic approach. He did not try to push the issue any further and consulted with the British instead. The British sent in troops, and a large British/Canadian army was assembled. They were sent some one thousand miles to the Red River region. In the meantime, Macdonald and Riel seemed to make good progress in their negotiations, and it seemed that perhaps a peaceful settlement could be arranged.

But as this was going on, Canadian settlers from the east began to cause trouble. This led Riel to take matters into his own hands and have people arrested. These actions led to him actually authorizing the execution of a man named Thomas Scott. Prime Minister Macdonald was appalled that Riel would attempt to assume such power over the region and become a one-man judge, jury, and executioner. So, Macdonald threw down the gauntlet and decided to dismantle Riel's provisional government by force.

As the large army approached, Riel's resistance all but collapsed. Riel himself took off over the border to hide in the United States. Even so, Prime Minister Macdonald was fairly benevolent when it came to the Métis who remained, providing generous tracts of land that were set aside specifically for the Métis.

The whole region, in the meantime, would become the Province of Manitoba with the Manitoba Act of July 15th, 1870. This was followed a year later by the joining of British Columbia to Canada proper in 1871. Prince Edward Island would also join the fold in the east in 1873. It seemed that Canada's own manifest destiny of reaching out from east to west was becoming a reality.

Prime Minister Macdonald seemed to have a lot of success stories to tell about his young nation. But average Canadians at the ballot box were ready for change all the same. And in 1873, the Macdonald government was replaced by the Liberal Party of Canada. Beyond simply being "against the conservatives," the Liberal Party did not seem to be too unified, and their agenda began to stall. Making matters worse, by 1874, Canada entered into a recession. This paved the way for Macdonald and his conservative government's return in the very next election. Macdonald ended up serving a second non-consecutive term in 1878.

One of the first things Macdonald's government did to change course was to enact high tariffs on imports, a move that began in 1879. These efforts managed to attract attention from overseas competitors, and they also created more industrial output at home. The populace was grateful for Macdonald's efforts, and he easily retained his prime minister post in 1882, 1887, and 1891.

Macdonald actually died in June of 1891, right after coming out on top in what would turn out to be his final successful election. His party would then have a succession of four different prime ministers at the helm of Canada's government before they lost their majority position in the election of 1896. That year, the liberal wing of Canadian politics was once again ushered into power with Prime Minister Wilfrid Laurier at its head.

Laurier was himself a milestone in that he was the first French Canadian to rise to the role of prime minister. Laurier was a stylish, neat, and trim man who impressed his peers with his impeccable English as well as his impeccable French. Laurier was a man who looked to the future and often proudly proclaimed that the "twentieth century belongs to Canada."

But the 20th century would bring things that neither Laurier nor many other Canadians could have imagined at the time. Once the year 1900 rolled around, Britain was still a power that spanned the globe, but cracks in this great empire were already beginning to emerge. War had broken out in South Africa between the British and the Dutch, leading to great disdain from the international community.

Nevertheless, the Canadians were tapped to join forces with the British in this struggle, and the British ultimately won in 1902. However, the empire was mired in controversy afterward. Many around the world questioned the tactics of the British in this engagement, and the victory itself was at least somewhat Pyrrhic in the sense that the British Empire racked up a huge number of casualties in order to achieve it. The British side, in fact, sustained nearly 100,000 casualties, twice as much as their opponents that they supposedly bested in the war.

Nevertheless, after the war, Canada entered into a boom period in which immigration from both the US and Europe increased. There was also a push into underpopulated territories, and by 1905, Canada had gained a couple more provinces with the establishment of Alberta and Saskatchewan. Interestingly enough, most of the settlers to converge onto these new provinces were not Canadian-born citizens but mostly immigrants from eastern Europe, such as Poles, Russians, and Ukrainians.

Canada would enter into a relatively productive and beneficial period, with its population rising to seven million. Life was good, but there were those who were disenchanted with the high price of some of the staple goods that Canada routinely imported. To alleviate this concern, in 1911, Laurier made an agreement with US President William Howard Taft to enter into a mutual tariff reduction.

Laurier and his party were confident that this accomplishment would ensure the continuation of their government through the next election cycle. They were wrong. Instead, many Canadians were put off by what they felt were policies that were too pro-American. And instead of riding on a tide of victory, Laurier and company were cast out on a tide of electoral defeat.

Politics can indeed be unpredictable at times, and as much as politicians think they can manipulate their constituents, they are occasionally thrown curveballs that they did not quite anticipate. Laurier's successor, the conservative Prime Minister Sir Robert Borden, would be thrown just such a curveball when the war to end all wars—World War One—took up most of his time in office.

Chapter 9 – Canada, Two World Wars, and a Cold One

"After two world wars, the collapse of fascism, Nazism, communism and colonialism and the end of the cold war, humanity has entered a new phase of its history."

-Hans Kung

The war to end all wars—as World War One (or the Great War) would come to be called—had been long in the making, but it was sparked by a single incident. A Serbian nationalist had assassinated the visiting archduke of Austria, Franz Ferdinand, and his wife in June 1914. This led to Austria seeking damages against Serbia. Eventually, Austria issued several demands, but one of them was so draconian that the Serbs knew to give in would essentially mean giving up their own autonomy. They refused to meet the unrealistic demands, and Austria prepared for war.

Austria's ally of Germany also made it clear that it, too, would fight. Even the Ottoman Empire—the sick man of Europe—sided with the Central Powers against Serbia. Serbia was not alone in this struggle, though, as it was able to rely on the might of its powerful ally Russia. After Russia joined, so did France and Great Britain. And with Britain drawn into World War One, the Canadians were brought along for the ride by default.

Even though Canada was basically an autonomous dominion, the one thing out of their control was major foreign policy decisions, and with a snap of their fingers, the British could have Canadians running to war. Fortunately for the British, the Canadians were fairly enthusiastic about the prospects of participating in this conflict. In all, some 425,000 Canadians would don military uniforms and join the fight in Europe.

Some of the most brutal fights would take place on the Western Front in Belgium and France, and one of the first major operations that the Canadian troops would take part in occurred in Ypres, Belgium, in the spring of 1915. One of the most thrilling moments for the Canadian troops occurred in April of 1917 when Canadian forces broke through a solid German line of defense at Vimy Ridge, leading the way for the Allied Forces.

However, as well as the Canadian deployments were doing, by 1917, the recruitment efforts in Canada proper had slowed down considerably. Fighting in the war had become a polarizing subject, and it was primarily the French Canadians who did not wish to be involved. It must be said that French Canadians have been somewhat notorious in their desire to remain neutral.

During both the American Revolution and the War of 1812, French Canadians sought to distance themselves from taking a side. The same can be said of World War One. And even when some tried to use their French heritage as a reason to join the war effort, they would not budge. Even though France was being invaded by Germany, it did not seem to mean too much for the average French Canadian, as they had become completely disconnected from their ancestral France centuries ago.

Nevertheless, among the segment of Canadians who did wish to serve, they served with distinction. The Canadians were also there for the climactic Battle of Mons in November of 1918, which saw the

German military's most decisive defeat. One of the top Canadian leaders during this struggle was a certain general named Sir Arthur Currie.

Interestingly enough, prior to the breakout of World War One, Currie was actually a real estate agent who happened to participate with a local Canadian militia in his off-time. But while his real estate career was lackluster at best, Currie's service as a military commander was absolutely outstanding. Currie led his troops during a time when the British and German forces were locked in a stalemate, literally dug into the trenches and popping up to fire at one another. Neither side was making any real progress.

It was up to Currie and his Canadian regiment to break through this stalemate. And after the Canadians broke through the German lines at Vimy Ridge, Currie was promoted to the position of "Inspector-General" for the Canadian Armed Forces.

Along with directly providing troops, Canada also contributed to the war effort on a monetary level, and it actually paid for British munitions in the final years of the conflict. Britain itself was put under great financial stress during the war, and as a result of Canada's role in aiding the British with money, the Canadians managed to rise from a junior partner to more of an equal on the world stage. When peace talks were carried out in Paris in 1919, Canada was treated as an equal, and it was even made a member of the newly established League of Nations.

After the war, Canada had grown considerably, both in its political stature and in its population, which had reached eight and a half million at this time. Its infrastructure had also greatly improved, with efficient railways connecting one side of the country to the other, as well as streetcars being readily available on the local level in cities. Roads for cars were also in development, as Canadian interest in automobiles began to increase.

In fact, Henry Ford (the founder of Ford Motor Company) set up shop right in Windsor, Ontario, and since Detroit was not far away, vehicles were not hard to find, at least for those with enough money to buy them. As good as things were going in Canada, the early 1920s saw yet another recession. It is important to note that this downturn in Canada occurred several years before the stock market crash of 1929, which would send shockwaves all over the globe.

Yes, even before the crash, Canada was still very much a country in transition, and Canadians were having financial difficulties. Many average Canadians who had left rural farms for the industrialized cities were suddenly having a hard time even finding a job. Canada's welfare system, which was put in place to help support those in need, was not up to capacity for the need that was present, and the Canadian government at this time was hesitant to expand social programs.

This sudden recession was over quickly, though, and postwar economic conditions quickly improved. Canadian products such as wheat and wood pulp were in demand, and Americans, in particular, were paying large sums of money for a steady supply of them. Canadian manufacturing, such as the aforementioned Ford plant in Windsor, also began to pick up steam, hiring droves of local factory workers in order to meet the demand for the steady production of goods.

Canadian cities also saw a construction boom, during which some of the earliest Canadian skyscrapers were built. These were not quite as massive as the ones that had sprouted up in American cities such as New York and Chicago, but the Canadian skylines of Montreal and Toronto featured towering buildings in the 1920s all the same. Mining in the Canadian Shield, which was far from the cities, was also highly profitable. With proceeds from projects such as these, Canada's government was finally able to decrease taxation on its people and begin to set aside funds to pay lingering debts from the war.

The prime minister during this boom period was a man by the name of William Lyon Mackenzie King. King was a charismatic firebrand of Canadian politics, and he was able to reach out to Anglo-Canadians and French Canadians alike. Being able to bridge this divide was important for King since he felt that the best way to have a strong and prosperous Canada was by healing the divisions of the past—primarily the historical division between French- and English-speaking Canadians.

King was sharp-witted, but he was ultimately a pragmatist, one who played for the long game rather than short-term success. King would maintain leadership throughout the rest of the 1920s, seeking stability above all else. Canadian stability would be severely challenged just like much of the rest of the world after the stock market crash of 1929 and the ensuing Great Depression of the early 1930s.

For Canada, the first and most immediate effect of the Depression was a drastic decline in one of the nation's staple agricultural crops—wheat. Canada had long made money through its wheat, which was primarily grown in the western provinces of Alberta, Saskatchewan, and Manitoba. Yet, at the start of the Great Depression, there was a wheat surplus, and people just were not buying as they had been. With this drop in demand for wheat, the price rapidly dropped until farmers could not make enough money to justify all the hard work they put into growing this heavily involved crop.

The next domino to fall was the wood pulp industry. Canada had long been supplying American cities with wood pulp for the production of paper. However, paper purchases also went into decline during the Depression, and soon the prices—and ultimately the profits—of pulp sank like a rock. This trend continued to affect all of Canada's industrial sectors.

The year 1930 had seen a return of the conservatives to power, with Prime Minister R. B. Bennett at the helm. Bennett sought to use the tariffs to break through Canada's stagnation. Or, as Bennett himself put it at the time, he would utilize tariffs "to blast a way into the markets of the world." Although tariffs might have worked under normal circumstances, the global Great Depression did not make for normal times, so his tariffs had very little effect.

Canada's saving grace came in 1932 when Britain agreed to lower rates of duty on all commerce conducted between members of the British Empire. These measures helped keep the Canadian economy afloat during these tough times.

The previous year, in 1931, Britain had also enacted the Statute of Westminster, which served to solidify Canada's independent status in the commonwealth. The statute, however, left one thin thread of coercive power on Britain's part, as it allowed the British Parliament the ability to amend the Canadian constitution. However, this could only be done with the consent of Canada's own parliament.

So, in some sense, full autonomy was a fine line in Canada at this point since, if, for whatever reason, the Canadian Parliament agreed on it, Britain could still intervene. Such a scenario, however, would seem highly unlikely. The statute also further cemented the dominion status of Newfoundland, which at this point was still being treated as a separate colony.

At any rate, independent or not, there was still the problem of widespread unemployment, and the Canadian government had to take action to try and put all of these suddenly idle hands to work. This was done largely through industrial projects, such as the construction of roads, railways, and other infrastructure. And if all else failed, some were even given the monotonous task of simply mowing grass in local city parks.

The situation was much different in rural communities, where farmers struggled both with poor economic conditions and poor soil due to bad droughts that occurred in 1936 and again in 1937. Making matters even worse, the drought came paired with a bad infestation of locusts, making the situation seem like a true tribulation for those who experienced it.

One of the most peculiar phenomena for rural folk during these days was the rise of Bennett buggies. Just what exactly was a Bennett buggy? Well, since gas prices were sky-high, folks had resorted to putting their cars in neutral and hitching horses to the otherwise useless vehicle to pull them into town! This was both an inventive and ironic fixture of the times. Most of these cars were purchased during the prosperous 1920s under Prime Minister Mackenzie King, yet in the 1930s, under Prime Minister Bennett, these once proud automobile owners had to pull a page from the past and transform their autos into horse-drawn buggies.

Bennett himself had his reckoning in the election of 1935, in which he and his party were thrown out almost entirely. Bennett was humiliated, and he left Canada altogether, heading to Great Britain to lick his wounds. Returning to lead the nation in his place was the former Prime Minister William Lyon Mackenzie King. The slogan during King's campaign was "It's King or Chaos." And many, remembering how successful King's steady hand was in the 1920s, believed it and chose King over what they perceived as absolute economic chaos in the land.

In truth, Bennett was partially a victim of circumstances out of his control. Bennett, of course, had no control over the stock market crash and the ensuing Great Depression, but his policies were certainly not as helpful as they could have been. And it was this perceived failure to respond to the pressing needs of Canadians that gave the Liberal Party all the opening they needed to surge once again to the top of Canadian politics.

However, once King was in office, he realized just what kind of trouble he had inherited. He had run on a platform of fixing what ailed the Canadian government, yet once in power, he struggled to find the right approach. And as he was stumbling to figure out what to do, international affairs proved to be a rather convenient distraction from troubles at home.

During the 1930s, dictators had come to prominence in many parts of the world. Germany was being led by Adolf Hitler and his Nazi Party. Japan was being run by a pro-military faction led by Japanese Prime Minister Hideki Tojo. And Italy had been in the grip of Italian fascists, with dictator Benito Mussolini at the head. The world community was intensely worried (and rightly so) about these developments, yet Mackenzie King, just like his British peer at the time—the infamous appeaser Neville Chamberlain—took a hands-off approach.

As early as 1935, when the League of Nations sanctioned Italy in condemnation of its invasion of Ethiopia, Canada refused to cooperate. And in 1937, while visiting London, King expressed Canada's lack of interest in foreign entanglements. From here, he actually went on to visit Hitler himself in Germany. Damningly enough, Canadian Prime Minister Mackenzie King even wrote about the Nazi leader in glowing terms, making him out to be a humble servant of the people or, as he put it, "a simple German peasant." At one point, King even referred to Hitler as being a kind of German version of Joan of Arc.

Of course, these musings of Mackenzie King would not age well, as this man whom he perceived as a champion of the common people would not only lead the world to war but would also be the principal architect and director of the worst atrocities ever committed in world history. Yet, at the same time, he did manage to tell Hitler that if war really did erupt, Canada would most certainly be backing the British.

King, in truth, was totally for British Prime Minister Neville Chamberlain's policies of appeasement. Like many others, King desperately wished to avoid war, and he was willing to appease the bullying tactics of fascist dictators in order to do so. As such, King fully approved when Neville went above and beyond to bend over backward for Hitler and all of his many demands as long as if it meant that bloodshed could be avoided. Along with visiting European heads of state, King also crafted a close relationship with US President Franklin Delano Roosevelt.

President Roosevelt—often simply referred to as F. D. R.—came into office at the height of the Great Depression just like Mackenzie King, and he quickly presented himself as the champion of the working class. He did this by using the power of the federal government to create major projects to get people back to work and to create safety nets for those who had fallen on hard times.

F. D. R. and King hit it off well enough, and the forward-thinking Roosevelt, who was already worried of a future world war, consciously considered close ties with Canada to be paramount for the sake of mutual defense of the North American continent. And in 1938, just on the eve of World War Two, the United States and Canada did indeed forge a mutual defense pact should they face an assault from an outside aggressor. The following year, in the fall of 1939, Germany launched a merciless attack, not on the US or Canada but on neighboring Poland.

Although Poland is far from the coasts of North America, this assault kickstarted what would quickly come to be called the Second World War. Britain, which had tried so hard to appease Hitler, was now forced to declare war on Germany. Britain's ally of France did so as well. Canada then came to the fold, officially declaring war on Germany on September 10th.

Even so, the United States did not feel obligated to do so. Yes, the US pledged to defend Canada if it were attacked, but the United States was not ready to declare war on a foreign power simply because Britain had. It would take a couple more years and a Japanese attack on American soil to finally get the United States to declare war on the Axis Powers of Germany, Italy, and Japan.

Mackenzie King, in the meantime, won the right to lead the government once again in the election of 1940, positioning him to be Canada's wartime leader. As would similarly be the case in the United States, once Canada was at war, its economic circumstances would change. Droves of Canadians were being hired to work in industrial plants and factories in order to supply the war effort. Canada would produce everything from bullets to aircraft for the Allied war machine. To further safeguard the wartime economy, Prime Minister King also made sure to establish wage and price controls to prevent any chance of inflation. The Canadians also had to commit themselves to a bit of sacrifice on the home front, as important goods for the war, such as rubber, coal, and even coffee, were being reduced to ration levels for the average Canadian citizen.

Nevertheless, due to the industry boom, Canadians were suddenly in a much better position economically speaking, with most of them being fully employed and making more money than ever before. And when the United States of America finally joined the conflict in late 1941, Canada was in a prime position to rev up the American war engine as well. The US, as it turns out, was a bit behind in armaments, so it was agreed to essentially bring the US and Canadian armament programs together in order to bring the United States better up to speed.

And as it pertains to the actual war overseas, Canada was indeed a valuable player, sending over a million troops to fight in both the European and Pacific theaters. Of this number, it is said that approximately 131,000 served in the Royal Canadian Air Force, fighting alongside the British and other Allies in daring air raids over Nazi-occupied Europe.

However, as intense as the fighting was in Europe, some of the most brutal engagements that the Canadian forces experienced were in the Pacific theater. In fact, around the same time that the United States was being attacked by Japan at Pearl Harbor, Hawaii, Canadians were desperately trying to fend off an invasion of Hong Kong. Although the city of Hong Kong is situated on the mainland of China, it was a British colony at that time.

Japan had been waging war with China since the early 1930s (since the 1931 Mukden Incident or Manchurian Incident, in fact), and after declaring war on Britain, all bets were off. The Canadian force in Hong Kong was a small one, and they were quickly overwhelmed by the Japanese invasion force. The Canadians stationed in Hong Kong ultimately ended up surrendering to the Japanese on December 25th, 1941—Christmas Day, no less.

Needless to say, it would not be a very good Christmas for these Canadian prisoners of war, and for the next four years, they would be at the mercy (or lack thereof) of the Japanese. But it was the Japanese attack at Pearl Harbor that would be the ultimate game-changer since it brought the previously hesitant United States into the war on the side of the Allies. Both Britain and Canada were immensely pleased that they could now rely upon the industrial juggernaut of the United States to back them in the war.

The Americans largely led the war from here on out, with Canadians and the British playing a backing role. A massive US invasion force landed in North Africa, leapfrogged to Sicily, and then invaded Italy. This rapid invasion prompted the Italians to surrender, knocking out the first of the three Axis Powers. The Canadians also served alongside the Americans when they took the fight directly to the Germans on D-Day, landing off the shores of Normandy, France, in June of 1944. These courageous Canadians braved machine gun nests in order to create a beachhead in continental Europe.

Germany would ultimately be defeated in May of 1945. The last holdout of the Axis would be Japan, which would not give up until the late summer of 1945. And they only did so after having two nuclear bombs dropped on them and after a very late-stage declaration of war by the Soviet Union. Yes, the Soviets, who had been fighting a desperate war against the Germans since 1941, did not actually declare war against the Japanese until August 9th, 1945. Japan officially surrendered on September 2nd.

Interestingly enough, the nuclear weapons deployed on Japan were the beneficiaries of uranium developed in Canada. The dropping of the atomic bombs on the Japanese cities of Nagasaki and Hiroshima still remains controversial to this day, but most historians believe that their use did indeed shorten what would have otherwise been a prolonged quagmire of guerilla warfare and ferocious battles if the Allies had attempted a conventional land invasion of Japan.

Regardless, the world was shocked by their use, and soon, with the development of the far more powerful hydrogen grade nuclear weapons, fear would grip both the US and Canada, as hydrogen bombs could suddenly fall on North America. Canada, which had worked closely with its US partner in the development of nuclear weapons, would have front row seats for the ensuing Cold War that followed.

Although the Soviet Union was ostensibly an ally of the United States, Canada, Britain, and the other Allied Powers during the war, shortly after their common enemies had been defeated, the relations between the Soviet Bloc and the Western powers began to frost over. There were almost immediate disagreements over what role the Soviets should play in postwar Europe, and after several land grabs by the Russians, British Prime Minister Winston Churchill famously stated that an "Iron Curtain" had descended across Europe.

These were prophetic words from a world power that soon saw a great decline. Yes, the fighting of World War Two took a terrible toll on Britain, and soon, it would be bereft of much of its empire. In the meantime, the United States, as well as Canada, took on a leading role. Canada was a leading member of the newly established United Nations, and it played a major part in the Cold War discussions over the dangers of nuclear weapons. In 1949, the Soviet Union exploded an atomic bomb of their own, thereby raising the stakes significantly.

The world was now dominated by two superpowers—the US and the USSR (the Union of Soviet Socialist Republics)—which both had nuclear weapons. As the arms race between these two nations commenced, the possibility of ending all human life on Earth became a possibility. This is exactly the sort of thing that the United Nations was (and still is) supposed to prevent. A commission, of which Canada was a part, had looked into a means of peaceful disarmament, but neither the US nor the USSR could agree on any feasible way of doing this.

As the Cold War gripped the world, heads of state in Canada realized they would have to work outside of the United Nations in order to find meaningful solutions. Thus, Canada joined the North Atlantic Treaty Organization (otherwise known as NATO). By grouping itself in a strategic alliance with both the United States and Britain, Canada was hoping to strengthen its military capabilities, as well as deter any would-be belligerence by the Soviets in the North Atlantic.

NATO made Canada puts its money where its mouth was since the treaty pledged that both Canada and the United States would immediately aid any NATO ally should they come into conflict with the Russians. This called for a massive military buildup on Canada's part, and by 1953, the Canadians were spending 45 percent of their budget on their military. The most important investment, however, would be in the complex early warning systems—radar installations—that would serve to warn not just Canada but also all of North America of an impending nuclear strike.

Canada would have three main installations—the Distant Early Warning Line located in the Arctic, the Mid-Canada Line, and the Pinetree Line, which was situated at Canada's forty-ninth parallel. These installations stood as silent sentinels during the Cold War to tip off Canada and, more importantly from a military sense, the nuclear-bomb-wielding United States that immediate action was necessary.

In reality, however, if the Soviets had lobbed nuclear missiles at North America, there was not a whole lot Canada or the US could do to prevent them from hitting their targets. The most that could be done in the brief amount of time that the early warning systems provided was simply to lob nuclear missiles right back at them. Since both parts of the world would be catastrophically destroyed in the process, such a thing seemed pointless—perhaps even a bit *mad*.

But "mutually assured destruction" (MAD), as they called it, was actually the name of the game. It was theorized that if the Soviets knew ahead of time that their attack would receive an equally devastating counterattack, they would be deterred from launching an attack in the first place. Yes, it seems crazy, but during the Cold War, it was crazy enough to work. This is demonstrated by the fact that nuclear war did not occur, and we are still here.

Chapter 10 – Canada at the Dawning of a New Millennium

"The northern border is a different problem set than our southern border. We're not going to put a fence between America and Canada, across Glacier Park. I grew up there. We can use some technological controls. We work with the Canadians more, and there's a lot of property we share, along with tribal lands."

-Ryan Zinke

By the late 1960s, Canada had truly come into its own. Not only was Canada independent of Great Britain and equipped with both a strong economy and military, but it had also forged its own unique national culture. This was—at least symbolically—demonstrated in 1965 when Canada established its own national flag, marked with the now-iconic red maple leaf.

Just about everyone born after 1965 can readily recognize the Canadian maple leaf flag. Yet, prior to this date, Canada had had a variety of flags, which all, in one way or another, paid homage to Britain's Union Jack. But the maple leaf, as unique and quirky as it might be, was something that Canada could finally call its own.

Another Canadian milestone that occurred in 1965 was the national implementation of Canada as a bilingual country. No longer would French speakers have to feel like second-class citizens. Nevertheless, it was in French-speaking Quebec that a movement toward Quebec independence began to take root. In 1967, with the Canadian centennial anniversary celebration of the 1867 independence through the British North America Act as a backdrop, some serious questions as to whether Quebec should hang on to the rest of Canada were being asked.

To mark the centennial, many heads of state from abroad arrived on Canadian soil, such as then US President Lyndon B. Johnson, Queen Elizabeth II of Britain, and President Charles de Gaulle of France. The most greatly anticipated among them was, no doubt, Charles de Gaulle, especially in light of the Quebec question.

De Gaulle visited Quebec, and rather than simply celebrating the centennial, he courted controversy by appearing to support Quebec's independence from Canada. De Gaulle gave a speech in French to an admiring crowd of French Canadians, in which he was heard to declare, "Vive le Québec libre!" These were not just words to wish the Quebec people well; it was a specific phrase that was used by Quebec residents who wished to separate from Canada. This was considered to be particularly troubling because France was a member of NATO and ostensibly a partner with Canada. Yet, de Gaulle's actions were little more than bluster since France was a weakening power and had very little clout on the world stage at this time.

Still, it was a hard pill for Canadian unionists to swallow. They could not believe that de Gaulle had, well, the gall to do such a thing. De Gaulle was subsequently condemned by Canadian authorities, and the brash French prime minister left shortly thereafter. However, some would wonder if the damage was already done.

In the late 1960s, radical separatist movements began to grow. And by 1970, a particularly nasty Quebec nationalist group, which called themselves Front de libération du Québec, or FLQ for short, was established. Although it is unclear what socialist or communist ties the FLQ may have had, it is worth noting that throughout the late 1960s and early 1970s, several communist-backed or inspired groups appeared all over the globe with similar names. For example, in the northern Ethiopian region of Tigray around this time, the TPLF, which stands for Tigray People's Liberation Front, was formed. Also, in the Middle East, Palestinian radicals formed the PLO or Palestinian Liberation Organization. Sudan also had a group called SPLM, which stood for Sudan People's Liberation Movement. These are just a few examples of the countless groups from this time period that have the words "people," "liberation," and "front" in their clumsy, unwieldy acronyms, and many had ties to the communist bloc, in one way or another.

At any rate, the French-Canadian radicals known as the FLQ were bad news for the federal government of Canada, and in the fall of 1970, they kicked off what was known as the October Crisis by inflicting several terrorist attacks against the Canadian government during that month.

During their rampage, the group actually abducted the British trade commissioner for Montreal. They ended up holding this man hostage and vowed not to free him until some of their own separatist colleagues who had been previously arrested were released. The Canadian government, of course, was not about to do any such thing. They had their hands full as it was; the last thing they needed was to set free even more radical separatists.

The group also strangely demanded that the Canadian government read their manifesto to the nation across broadcast media, as if such a thing would help their struggle. On top of this, there was also a request for a large amount of cash and an escort to a "friendly country." Predictably enough, the federal government of Canada declined to do any of these things.

Once the FLQ radicals knew that Canadian officials would not negotiate with terrorists, the separatists tried to do even more damage by taking Quebec's labor minister—Pierre Laporte—hostage. This time, it was the provincial government of Canada that became distressed enough to invite more draconian tactics to be used by the federal government. The local Quebec government requested Prime Minister Pierre Elliott Trudeau to intervene by sending in troops.

An alarmed Trudeau, fearing that Quebec's provincial government just might disintegrate in the chaos, obliged this request. Both the military and police worked together to capture the terrorists, but unfortunately for the abducted labor minister, his fate was already sealed—he was killed by his captors. The British trade commissioner fared much better, gaining his freedom from his captors in December of 1970, just in time for Christmas.

Although the threat of the October Crisis was waged by a relatively small group of people, their tactics were so devastating that this incident ranks as one of the greatest threats to Canadian sovereignty of all time. Canadian officials afterward learned to play hardball with terrorists, and future would-be agitators seemed to get the message. For the rest of the 1970s, Canada's domestic affairs remained relatively quiet and stable.

This stability came just in time since Montreal was scheduled to host the Olympics in 1976. The show went on without much of a hitch, except for the faulty design of Montreal's stadium, which boasted a retractable roof that did not seem to work all too well.

But that same year, a movement for separatism was once again beginning to take up steam; at least it did so quietly this time around. This movement was not a violent radical terrorist group of French Canadians but rather a provincial political party that sought reform and possibly future separation, not through bullets but rather ballots. The group, which called itself the Parti Québécois, gained power in Quebec in November of 1976. One of the first things that the Parti Québécois did was institute mandatory French in public institutions in

Quebec. Street signs were in French, emergency services required French, and so on and so forth.

The most immediate result of this legislation was an exodus of English-speaking Canadians out of Quebec. Rather than taking the time to learn some French, these English-speaking Canadians decided to move to another province where English still reigned supreme. This was not good for Quebec in the long run since Quebec was sparsely inhabited and still struggling to bolster a decent-sized population.

But the greatest development of the Parti Québécois was the creation of a referendum in which residents of Quebec could actually vote on whether or not to leave Canada proper. This referendum was ultimately held in 1980. The referendum failed, with only 40 percent voting to leave Canada and the other 60 percent voting to stay. Nevertheless, the very fact that Quebec would vote on secession sent shockwaves throughout the rest of Canada.

Besides this referendum, the next most consequential moment for Canada in the 1980s came with the introduction of the Canada Act in the year 1982. This act served as the final step in Canada's long march to full independence. This act formally ended the ability of the British government to amend the Canadian constitution at the "request and consent" of the Canadian Parliament. Now—no matter what—the only ones who could change the Canadian constitution were Canadians.

The only connection to Britain left intact was the fact that Queen Elizabeth II was still recognized as the monarch. But as is the case in Britain itself, this role is primarily a ceremonial one, with the true power of government laying in the parliament. The queen ultimately came to Canada herself to sign off on the act, which was made official on April 17th, 1982.

By 1985, a new Canadian prime minister—a conservative—by the name of Brian Mulroney was actively courting powerful new trade agreements with US President Ronald Reagan. Reagan also liked the idea, and he sought to establish a better trade deal between the United

States and both Canada and Mexico. The first step of this new partnership with Canada was made in October of 1987 when tariffs between the United States and Canada were removed for what was slated to be a ten-year time period. They also established a bilateral panel in which the two partners could oversee the whole process to make sure it was being conducted appropriately.

As many readers may very well guess, it was these measures that began the push toward what would become NAFTA (the North American Free Trade Agreement). It might surprise many, but Prime Minister Mulroney initially received some severe pushback from the idea of an economic trade union with the United States, with some suggesting that this was only the beginning of a more permanent political union. The concept might almost sound absurd, but for Canadians who long feared being annexed by the United States, their suspicions were real. Nevertheless, Brian Mulroney and Ronald Reagan formalized the deal on January 1st, 1989.

Prime Minister Mulroney began to lose favor, and he stepped down from politics in 1993, paving the way for Kim Campbell—Canada's first female prime minister—to take the helm in his place. Mulroney and Campbell's party would lose power in the election that took place later that fall, and the new government would be led by the liberal Jean Chrétien.

The rise of Jean Chrétien coincided with the rise of President Bill Clinton in the United States. Clinton would turn out to be a big supporter of free trade between the US and Canada, and he made sure that NAFTA was the law of the land, signing off on it on December 8th, 1993.

After putting NAFTA to bed, the next major political upheaval in Canada involved a second referendum on Quebec. Consequentially enough, many in Quebec were unhappy with NAFTA, thinking that the economic controls of the deal would have an adverse effect on local Quebec business. This referendum was held in 1995, and it managed to produce a startlingly much closer verdict. The campaign for this referendum touted as "Oui ou Non?" asked a simple question of Quebec residents—do you wish to stay in Canada? Yes, or no? It was a nail-biter—50.6 percent chose to stay part of Canada, while 49.4 percent of voters in Quebec voted to leave.

Prime Minister Jean Chrétien's party would manage to come out on top in the 2000 election, ensuring that his agenda would make it into the next millennium. Jean Chrétien would be prime minister when the United States was struck by the horrific terrorist attacks of September 11th, 2001. These attacks were launched by the terror group Al-Qaeda, who were being protected and given a safe haven by the Taliban of Afghanistan.

This attack sparked a US-led invasion of Afghanistan, and the subsequent occupation would last for twenty years before the US withdrew in August of 2021. Canadian troops were sent right alongside Americans to participate in this conflict. However, Canadians would not participate when the United States decided to go to war with Iraq under the false pretenses that Saddam Hussein had weapons of mass destruction (WMDs).

The case for WMDs in Iraq was famously made by George W. Bush's Secretary of State Colin Powell, who claimed that it was just a matter of time before Iraq had the capacity to attack the US with its WMDs. These claims were thought to be ludicrous by some at the time, and they were ultimately proven to be so. Canada, for one, was not buying it, and it declined to participate in the US invasion the Americans called Operation Iraqi Freedom.

However, Canadians did participate in NATO efforts to intervene in the Libyan Civil War. This is something that many Canadians now view as a mistake, perhaps of similar proportions to the misguided invasion of Iraq. After all, it was disruptions in the governments in Libya, Egypt, Iraq, and Syria that helped to pave the way for the rise of ISIS (Islamic State of Iraq and Syria).

ISIS, a group that has been condemned by none other than Al-Qaeda for being "too extreme," unleashed abuses upon civilian populations that have not been seen since the Middle Ages. ISIS members proved how intolerant they were by rampaging through much of the Middle East and killing and enslaving anyone who was not exactly like them. Even Muslims were slaughtered if the members of ISIS believed them not to be "their brand of Muslim."

Canada, like much of the rest of the world, saw the pure evil of ISIS for what it was. Canada readily supplied its troops to help combat this menace.

In the meantime, Canada entered into a new era in 2015 with the rise of Justin Trudeau as the new prime minister and the face of the Liberal Party of Canada. Trudeau is also the son of former Prime Minister Pierre Elliott Trudeau, establishing what many see as a Canadian political dynasty. Justin Trudeau was ushered into office with a pledge to decrease the tax burden on middle-class Canadian families while simultaneously increasing the tax responsibilities of the richest taxpayers in Canada. With the extra tax revenue from Canada's wealthiest earners, Trudeau was able to increase social programs for the average Canadian citizen.

Another major pledge of Prime Minister Justin Trudeau's government was to improve the situation of Canada's First Nations residents. Another highlight of his first term was the introduction of the controversial medically assisted dying provisions of 2016. This bit of legislation essentially allowed for assisted suicide for those who were suffering from incurable, terminal conditions.

In 2018, Prime Minister Trudeau also made waves when he made marijuana use completely legal throughout Canada with the passing of the Cannabis Act. This made Canada the second nation—after Uruguay—and the first G7 country to officially legalize the use of marijuana.

In 2020, Justin Trudeau participated in the forging of a revised and updated NAFTA-styled trade agreement called the United States-Mexico-Canada Agreement, or USMCA for short. It was around the time of this milestone that Canada—like much of the rest of the world—was being rocked by a global pandemic.

Justin Trudeau's party went on to retain their majority in Canada's election in 2021, but it was an uphill climb. The election took place in the midst of the botched US withdrawal from Afghanistan. The centralized government of Afghanistan, which had long been propped by the US and its British and Canadian allies, collapsed in stunning fashion, as the Taliban soon took it over. Prime Minister Justin Trudeau, just like US President Joe Biden, was criticized for how these things transpired under his watch. Critics and supporters of Justin Trudeau, of course, greatly differ on just how much blame Trudeau should take. But nevertheless, Justin Trudeau and his party prevailed. Prime Minister Justin Trudeau—as of this writing—continues to lead Canada to this very day.

Conclusion – O Canada! O Canada!

Canada has an incredible history, yet it is a history that often goes unnoticed. Canada, of course, has long lived in the shadow of other great powers. First, Canada was overshadowed by its early French colonizers. Once the British subdued the land of Canada, it would be the might of the British Empire that would obscure our view of true Canadian history.

Once Britain subsided in influence during the Cold War, the United States, as the dominant military and political force in North America, took the front seat, and Canada continued to remain in the background to much of the rest of the outside world. But while these juggernauts strode the world stage, Canadians have lived a rich and unique history all their own.

Canada can recount its history from the first of the First Nations people to cross the Bering Strait some fifteen thousand years ago, to the French fur trappers who dared to call early, icy settlements such as Port Royal home, and to the Canadians who immigrated from Britain and ended up becoming true trailblazers as they pushed westward through wild and rugged terrain to reach the western shores of the North American continent.

The story of Canada is not just the story of one group of people but of many. Those who live in Canada have a deep ancestry that traces to all over the globe, yet they have come together to forge something truly unique. The living standards and resources of Canada continue to rival much of the rest of the world; in fact, Canada is consistently listed as one of the best places to live. In April of 2021, in the annual "Best Countries Report," Canada was actually ranked as the number one country in which to live. If you are a resident of Canada, you most likely have excellent work opportunities and a top-notch quality of "life and social purpose." Canada was also seen as being a leader in social justice, something that has become increasingly important to many all over the world.

So having said that, if you can handle some lower temperatures, Canada is indeed a nice place to lay your head! O Canada! O Canada! It is a country with a great history and a great place to live!

Here's another book by Captivating History that you might like

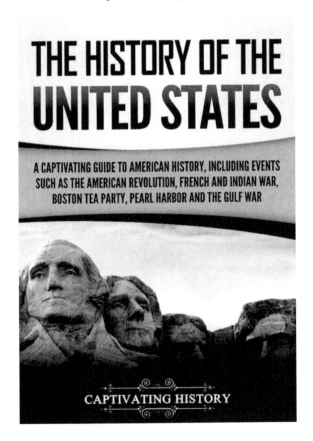

Free Bonus from Captivating History (Available for a Limited time)

Hi History Lovers!

Now you have a chance to join our exclusive history list so you can get your first history ebook for free as well as discounts and a potential to get more history books for free! Simply visit the link below to join.

Captivatinghistory.com/ebook

Also, make sure to follow us on Facebook, Twitter and Youtube by searching for Captivating History.

Appendix A: Further Reading and Reference

A Traveler's History of Canada. Robert Bothwell. 2001.

How Canada Came to Be: A Brief History. Anna Jennings Steen. 2017.

The History of Canada. Kenneth McNaught. 1991.

Printed in Great Britain
by Amazon

26940668R00056